MW01129774

# FIRST AND TEN

# FIRST AND TEN

*A Fresh Look at the Cleveland Browns*

## VINCE McKEE

ROWMAN & LITTLEFIELD
*Lanham • Boulder • New York • London*

Published by Rowman & Littlefield
An imprint of The Rowman & Littlefield Publishing Group, Inc.
4501 Forbes Boulevard, Suite 200, Lanham, Maryland 20706
www.rowman.com

86-90 Paul Street, London EC2A 4NE, United Kingdom

British Library Cataloguing in Publication Information Available

**Library of Congress Cataloging-in-Publication Data**
Names: McKee, Vince, author. Title: First and ten : a fresh look at the Cleveland Browns / Vince McKee.
Other titles: 1st and 10
Description: Lanham, Maryland : Rowman & Littlefield, [2023] | Includes bibliographical references and index. | Summary: "No matter the amount of losses, dysfunction, or controversy, the Cleveland Browns remain one of the most popular franchises in professional football. First and Ten covers the 'new' history of the Browns after their return to the NFL in 1999, focusing on the positives without shying away from the negatives, for a fresh look at this storied team"— Provided by publisher.
Identifiers: LCCN 2022061391 | ISBN 9781538179949 (cloth : acid-free paper) | ISBN 9781538179956 (epub)
Subjects: LCSH: Cleveland Browns (Football team : 1999- )—History. | Football—Ohio— Cleveland—History. | National Football League—History.
Classification: LCC GV956.C6 M35 2023 | DDC 796.332/640977132—dc23/eng/20230202
LC record available at https://lccn.loc.gov/2022061391

♾™ The paper used in this publication meets the minimum requirements of American National Standard for Information Sciences—Permanence of Paper for Printed Library Materials, ANSI/ NISO Z39.48-1992.

*This book dedicated to my late great grandfather Joe DeLuca up in heaven. He was the biggest Browns fan I have ever met. He told everyone he knew about being at the first Browns game in 1946 and the countless memories he shared growing up watching Paul Brown coach. No one, and I mean no one, was ever as smart as he was when it came to the accurate history of the franchise. This one is for you, Grandpa!*

# CONTENTS

# Acknowledgments

Thank you to my wife, Emily, and daughters, Maggie and Madelyn. You remain my everything and reason for breathing. I love you three more each and every day and I'm so proud of all three of you. Without you in my life, I could never do what I do or have the drive to do it. I miss you all every single minute I spend in the press box, sidelines, or announce table courtside. It is your love and support that makes it possible and enjoyable! While others may head to bars, parties, or other gatherings after games, I cannot wait to race home to you!

I would also like to thank my staff at Kee On Sports who sacrifice their time with friends and family to cover games. Kee On Sports is not just me; it is a total team effort and your contributions to it make us what we are today.

I want to thank my parents, Don and Maria McKee, and also my wife's parents, Bob and Debbie Lamb. With your willingness to watch the kids, I was able to leave to cover games earlier than I may have been able to at times. Also, you understand why I may not always be there on time or at a family function at all sometimes; this is a passion that doesn't check other people's personal schedules, and you get the fact that being a sportswriter and also being a great dad is a 24/7/365 job. I take both very seriously.

To the late great James Friguglietti who passed in March 2018. While others didn't have time to read a single word, you edited every one when I first started writing HERO ten-plus years ago. One cent of your knowledge was worth more than a million dollars out of your pocket. I'll never forget how much you helped me every step of the way. That in itself is worth far more than any dollar value.

Last but always first, thank you to my lord and savior Jesus Christ. It is through your work that all light is shed and peace is obtained.

# Note from the Author

I have been a Browns fan since I was old enough to remember watching sports. For me, my first Browns memory was the thrilling double over-time victory over the New York Jets in the Divisional Round of the AFC Playoffs following the 1986 regular season. It happened just days before my fifth birthday and it was my first real taste of sports joy. Sadly, no one ever talks about that game and the 489-yard passing performance of Bernie Kosar during the improbable comeback.

Instead, the national media always wanted to focus on John Elway's drive the following week that cost Cleveland a trip to the Superbowl. I have already written the book and read numerous books talking about The Drive, The Fumble, The Move, and so on down the miserable list. Why? Enough with the gloom and doom all the time when it comes to being a Browns fan.

There is only a handful of books about the Browns since they returned to the NFL in 1999, and the bulk of those focus on the failures of the franchise. While this book will touch on the struggles of the rebirth, it will focus on the brighter moments as well. I hope everyone enjoys this fresh look at what it means to be a Browns fan and why there are Browns Backers groups all over the world. It is not always easy being a Cleveland Browns fan, but no one does fandom better than those loyal to the Orange and Brown.

And yes, there are some stories in the book about when Bernie Kosar was here, but because 99.9 percent of Browns books are about that eight-year stretch when he was with the franchise, I wanted this book to be brand new, and give the fans a chance to be happy without it always being followed by, "What if." Enjoy and take pride in being a Browns fan again!

# Introduction

Cleveland is a blue-collar city with hardworking people who want to support their hardworking teams. No matter the previous season's record, the loyal fan base is confident that this will be their season. Times have been tough for Cleveland sports teams, but it wasn't always that way. In fact, in the late 1940s, all of the 1950s, and the early 1960s, Cleveland was the marquee sports city on the planet.

The story of the Orange and Brown dates back to 1946 when owner Mickey McBride formed the team and hired the legendary coach Paul Brown to win several championships and begin a dynasty that is still respected seventy-plus years later. Under the reign of Paul Brown, the Cleveland franchise won the AAFC championship four times: in 1946, 1947, 1948, and 1949. Their dominance upon entering the NFL was just as good, as they won the NFL Championship in 1950, 1954, and 1955. In the earliest days of professional football, the Cleveland Browns were the most coveted and respected franchise in existence.

They rebounded from a brief spell away from the playoffs in the 1970s, to give fans one of the most thrilling seasons in franchise history with the Kardiac Kids in 1980. Years later, the excitement would return as a hometown boy in Bernie Kosar would skip the NFL Draft just for the chance to play for the franchise he loved. With Bernie, the Browns appeared in three AFC Championship games in five years as Cleveland truly became "Browns Town!"

When Bill Belichick arrived in Cleveland, that spelled the end of Bernie Kosar under center. What few people realize is just how good a team Belichick built, including a playoff win, before the team bolted for Baltimore.

Upon their return to the league, the Browns have had several winning seasons, and numerous runs toward the playoffs, including 2002, 2007, and 2020. This book covers all of the fun, and sometimes dysfunction, of one of the most beloved franchises in NFL history since their return to the NFL in 1999.

This is a tale for every Browns fan who wears their Orange and Brown proudly every Sunday, no matter the team's record!

# PART I

# MOVING ON

*The Browns After Art Modell*

# Chapter 1

# A New Era Begins

BEFORE WE LOOK AT THE "NEW BROWNS," IT IS VITAL TO THIS TALE that we take one look back to how the old Browns ended, the franchise that is beloved all over the world. With Paul Brown coaching the original Cleveland Browns from 1946–1962, they won three NFL Championships, four AAFC Championships, and were year in, year out, one of the best teams in professional football.

It was easy to be a Cleveland Browns fan; everyone wanted to be one and so over the years the fandom grew. If it wasn't the Kardiac Kids of the early 1980s or the Bernie Kosar Browns of the late 1980s, the Orange and Brown provided so many great memories for their fans. Between multiple trips to the playoffs, including three trips to the AFC Championship game between 1986–1989, the Browns were a coveted franchise for any player. It seemed as though these glory days would never end, until an owner decided to change all of that and shock the world in November of 1995 with an announcement no one saw coming.

Arthur B. Modell was born on June 23, 1925. He was born into a Jewish family living in Brooklyn, New York. His father George was a once-prominent wine salesman, until the fatal stock market crash of 1929, when his business failed miserably as result of the crash. His father passed away when Art was only fourteen years of age. This horrible tragedy forced the young Modell to drop out of school get a job to support his family. He came from humble beginnings, making ends meet by cleaning the hulls at shipyards. It was also at this young age that Modell learned to do whatever was necessary to survive in any situation.

Modell was a true patriot and loved his country; he showed as much when he turned eighteen by joining the US Army Air Corps. He left the military following the completion of World War II. The young and ambitious Modell decided to enroll in a New York City television school with the help of the GI Bill. He began his first foray into ownership when he went on to form his own production company with a fellow student in 1947.

Only two years into the business, Modell was quickly met with success when in 1949, they produced one of the first daytime shows in the country, *Market Melodies*. It was a show dedicated to cooking and decorating. In 1954, using the lucrative Grand Union account as leverage, he was hired as a senior account executive at the advertising company L. H. Hartman Co. in New York City, eventually becoming a partner. Modell continued to expand and grow his brand, fifty years before the term was used on the frequent basis it is today.

His passion for ownership and taking control of business ventures grew even more as he spent the majority of the 1950s working in public relations and television production in New York City. He wanted to get his hands on as many things as possible and see how every aspect of television and marketing worked. He had a bigger plan in mind all along. It was in 1961 that Modell took his love of business and put that same passion into sports. With the accompaniment of a few others, he purchased the Cleveland Browns. He borrowed nearly three million dollars, and found partners to cover the rest of the purchase. The Browns were already a very successful franchise at this point with an incredible head coach and the investment was a sound one for Modell and his associates.

It didn't take Modell long into his time in ownership to anger fans and cause havoc in the organization. Original coach Paul Brown had already led the Cleveland Browns to eleven straight title games, but that wasn't good enough for Art Modell. In a power play, Modell fired Brown on January 9, 1964. It was done in the middle of a newspaper strike and went down as one of the most shocking moments in Cleveland sports history.

After firing Brown, Modell quickly named Brown's assistant, Blanton Collier, as the new coach on January 16, 1963. Paul Brown had lost control of the team because of Jim Brown's horrible antics in the locker room that caused turmoil. Instead of sticking by the legendary coach, Modell sided with the player and fired one of the greatest coaches in the history of sports.

Fans were irate and players who loved Paul Brown were confused, but Modell was brash and determined to do things his way. In 1964 the Browns finished 10–3–1 and appeared in the 1964 NFL Championship Game against a heavily favored Don Shula coached Baltimore Colts team. The Browns beat the Colts 27–0 in Cleveland Municipal Stadium. This particular Browns team consisted of many players initially drafted and acquired by Paul Brown. It was Paul Brown's team that won the championship, not the newly appointed owner Modell.

Over the next thirty years in Cleveland, not a single Modell team won the league title. Prior to Modell's arrival, the Browns had dominated the NFL and the AAFC, winning seven championships in seventeen years. They fired a proven winner in Paul Brown, and Modell slowly began to run the team down the tubes after that.

Despite the chaos Modell was creating in Cleveland, he was doing positives for the NFL as a whole. He carried with him a past talent for promotions and used that skill to start many new innovations in the NFL. He began by scheduling pro football preseason doubleheaders at Cleveland Stadium. He was a genius when it came to using his assets to create more money. Modell didn't hesitate to provide his team as an opponent for both the first prime time Thanksgiving game in 1966 and the opening Monday Night Football broadcast in 1970. Many historians give Modell full credit for inventing Monday Night Football.

He continued to live the life of glamour and power when he married Patricia Breslin in 1969. Modell took an active role in the Cleveland community life and was a leader in fundraising for numerous charities. He also got behind and financially supported various Republican Party candidates. He made sure to be man around town and place his mark on many things.

Despite all the mistakes he would go on to make in his career, no one can ever dispute his passion for what he did and his true commitment to the community. It was, however, only a matter of time before his love of the almighty dollar took control over most if not all of his decisions.

He was also no stranger to controversy. In 1967, five African American members of the Browns were involved in a contract dispute and refused to report to training camp. Modell eventually traded or released four of the players, with only standout running back Leroy Kelly staying. It was yet another way that Modell was slowly starting to anger fans and players alike.

In 1973, Art Modell signed a twenty-five-year lease to operate Cleveland Stadium. Modell's newly formed company, Stadium Corporation, assumed the expenses of operations from the city, freeing up tax dollars for other purposes. Also, Modell would pay an annual rent of $150,000 for the first five years and $200,000 afterward to the city. In exchange, Modell would receive all revenue generated by the stadium. This was a giant steal for Modell when you factor in all the things that generated money for the stadium. Not only did they have a major league baseball team playing there in the Cleveland Indians, but when you factor in the countless concerts and other events at the stadium, this deal was huge.

Stadium Corp. invested in improvements, including new electronic scoreboards and luxury suites. It didn't take Modell long to anger the Cleveland Indians' ownership, as Modell did not share the league revenues earned from baseball games with the Indians. However, at the same time, he was the only one paying the yearly rent of $150,000.

In 1979, Modell was once again the centerpiece for controversy when he and Stadium Corp. were implicated in a lawsuit brought by Browns minority shareholder Robert Gries of Gries Sports Enterprises, who successfully alleged that Stadium Corp. manipulated the Browns' accounting records to help Stadium Corp. and Modell absorb a loss on real estate property that had been purchased in the Cleveland suburb of Strongsville as a potential site for a new stadium.

Despite the team's recent success in the mid and late 1980s, Modell continued to claim that he was losing money. He allowed the stadium to be rented out for the Belkin Concert Series run by Jules Belkin. The World Series of Rock was a recurring, day-long, and usually multi-act summer rock concert held outdoors at Cleveland Stadium in Cleveland, Ohio, from 1974 through 1980. It was popular enough to drive in 88,000 fans at times and this should have helped Modell generate money for the stadium; however, he just complained that it tore up his field. Stadium officials allowed fans to congregate near the stage on the playing field, which required fixing the turf before the Indians returned home.

After the 1975 football season, groundskeepers completely resurfaced the field, and installed a drainage system, to repair damage from the rock concerts. This, too, cost Modell even more money.

By the time Art Modell hired Bill Belicheck, Modell was still losing money despite solid attendance, and he was scrapping to find money to repair the fields and stands. Things went from bad to worse for Modell when, in May 1990, the Cuyahoga County voters approved a fifteen-year "sin tax" on alcohol and cigarette sales to finance the new Gateway Sports and Entertainment Complex. Construction started eighteen months later and the new era in Cleveland baseball began on the corner of Carnegie and Ontario in downtown Cleveland. Modell had now lost his biggest tenant and was left to occupy the aging building by himself as most concerts would move into the Gun Arena, and not be held at the stadium. Modell quickly went to the city to complain and to try to get the money to repair his stadium or get a brand new stadium.

Stadium Corp.'s suite revenues declined sharply when the Indians moved from the stadium to Jacobs Field in 1994; combined with rising player costs and deficits, it contributed to Modell's financial issues. Modell lost $21 million between 1993 and 1994. When Modell realized how much revenue he lost from the Indians moving out of Cleveland Stadium, he requested an issue be placed on the ballot to provide $175 million in tax dollars to refurbish the outmoded and declining Cleveland Stadium. He was denied, and things just continued to get worse.

This is where the biggest disagreement comes from many fans and media who were familiar with the situation at the time. The fans and residents of Cleveland were not obligated to spend their tax dollars on rebuilding an aging Cleveland Municipal Stadium, or even having the money spent on a new stadium. The issue with Modell was, he saw all the funding from the taxpayers going toward the Cavs and Indians, to both get brand-new facilities, and yet, his franchise was being left out in the cold. Fans and media alike can argue about this for the next 100 years, but the bottom line is, Modell was angry because he saw the other two teams in town get treated like royalty and his beloved Browns get neglected. If the city of Cleveland and its taxpayers would have agreed to build him a new home, or fix the current stadium, who knows if what was soon to happen would have actually occurred.

The city of Cleveland was in a state of resurgence, with a total rebirth to the downtown area. They built two beautiful new venues and left out Art Modell and the Browns. His overall fan rating continued to plummet as well, as he allowed Bill Belichick to cut fan-favorite quarterback Bernie Kosar from the team. The Browns couldn't seem to do anything right and they missed the playoffs for the fourth straight year after cutting Kosar. Despite finally returning to the playoffs in 1994, Modell was just about tapped out of funds when the city of Baltimore came calling with an offer he couldn't refuse.

It was then that the unthinkable happened. Modell still had time left on his lease but chose to ignore that and make the decision that no one saw coming, a decision that stunned not only the Cleveland sports fans but the entire sporting world. The Browns were a staple of the NFL and had one of the strongest fan bases in all of sports; however, none of that mattered.

Modell announced on November 6, 1995, that he had signed a deal to relocate the Browns to Baltimore in 1996. The very next day, on November 7, 1995, Cleveland voters overwhelmingly approved an issue that had been placed on the ballot at Modell's request, before he made his decision to move the franchise, which provided $175 million in tax dollars to refurbish the outdated and declining Cleveland Municipal Stadium. The tax bill being passed was not enough to convince Modell to stay. It was too little too late.

Art Modell made the announcement that shocked the sports world. He was moving one of the most beloved sports franchises in the history of sports away from their home city and their passionate fans. It was the bitter end of a reign that began nearly fifty years earlier when Modell bought the team.

The fans and city officials were outraged, as their beloved Browns were about to leave town and leave the city devoid of football. Virtually all of the team's sponsors pulled their support, leaving Cleveland Stadium devoid of advertising during the team's final weeks. Cleveland filed an injunction to keep the Browns in the city until at least 1998, while several other lawsuits were filed by fans and ticket holders. Despite all the rallies and protests, it simply didn't matter—the NFL was not about to block the move.

Cleveland finally caught a break and accepted a settlement that allowed the team to move to Baltimore but they would keep the rights to the name and the colors. On February 9, 1996, the NFL announced that the Browns would be "deactivated" for three years and that a new stadium would be built for a new Browns team. Either an expansion team or a team moved from another city would begin play in Cleveland in 1999. Modell would in turn be granted a new franchise for Baltimore, retaining the current contracts of players and personnel. The reactivated team for Cleveland would keep the Browns' name, colors, history, records, awards, and archives.

An expansion team was thrown at Cleveland at almost the last minute, and the new team never truly got things off the ground. Cleveland had to rush to build a stadium, and the NFL gave the new front office little time to create a roster. This included limited time for scouting and limited prestige to begin with in the NFL free agency market.

The bottom line was that they had to start over with Al Lerner as their new owner. This was a man who many forgot was with Modell on the first plane ride to Baltimore in 1995 when he was minority owner of the Cleveland Browns as they moved to become the Baltimore Ravens. Fans were so thrilled to have a team again, with the original name and colors, that they didn't bother looking into the past of Lerner and his major involvement with Art Modell.

Lerner was a former Marine who got into the banking industry as his first major venture following his time spent in the military. With his quick wit, humble nature, and incredible work ethic, Lerner became a major shareholder in MNC Financial in 1990. It was the parent corporation of Maryland National Bank, which was the largest bank headquartered in the entire state of Maryland. After taking over control, he made MNBA public in 1991 and never looked back as he built it into one of the largest banking companies in the entire world.

He wasn't done there, however. He would expand his portfolio once again as he bought and rented out more than 15,000 apartment units in the mid-Atlantic region. Already a banking billionaire and real estate tycoon, Lerner then reached out to Art Modell and purchased a 5 percent stake in the old Cleveland Browns franchise. Furthermore, in 1995, Lerner introduced Modell to Baltimore financiers of the deal, and he sat behind him on the podium at the press conference as Modell announced the team's move. Perhaps the worst salt in the wound was the fact that Modell actually signed the deal to move the Browns to Baltimore while sitting in a secret meeting on Lerner's personal jet.

In 1997, Modell paid $32 million to buy out Lerner's stake in the Baltimore Ravens, which had grown to 9 percent. Lerner then turned around and used that $32 million toward his purchase of the Browns.

Despite Lerner's past with Modell, he was beloved in Cleveland for two major reasons: He brought football back to the town that adored it and he was generally considered an incredible human being. Lerner was beloved by his employees who routinely rated MNBA as one of the most employee-friendly companies to work for in the world. He was generous with paychecks, health insurance, and just an overall amazing person to work for.

He was also a true humanitarian who did a lot for his country and then kept that tradition alive in his later years with incredible donations to charity. His most notable and largest donations went to the Cleveland Clinic and his alma mater, Columbia University. He was president of the Cleveland Clinic Foundation and donated over $100 million to the hospital system to establish the Cleveland Clinic Lerner College of Medicine at Case Western Reserve University School of Medicine. Lerner's estate also donated $10 million toward the construction of the National Museum of the Marine Corps.

Lerner donated approximately $25 million toward the construction of a new Columbia University student center in 1999, which was named Alfred Lerner Hall in his honor. He cared about students, he cared about his employees, and he cared about the football fans of Cleveland. Sadly, what he did for employees and students, he couldn't replicate for the hardworking and diehard football fans of Cleveland as it was one year of misery after another, thanks in part to a completely fumbled start to the new organization.

Part of the problem with the 1999 Browns was the rushed hiring of everyone, including the new president and CEO Carmen Policy, who seemed like the perfect fit. While working for nearly twenty years with the San Francisco 49ers, Policy was part of numerous Vince Lombardi Trophies. Doing everything from being special counsel to running the team, he was a part of five Super Bowl wins.

Not only did he come with championship pedigree, but he was also a hometown guy! Policy was a native of Youngstown, Ohio. In fact, he graduated in 1963 from Youngstown University before going into the legal field.

Things were going great for a while in San Francisco before his partnership with 49ers owner Eddie DeBartolo was terminated in the late 1990s. Policy wanted more credit for his part in the 49ers' successes, and Lerner was willing to give it to him in Cleveland. Well, everything except wins, as they proved pretty hard to come by.

If Al Lerner's biggest mistake was trusting Carmen Policy to hire the right people, then Policy's biggest mistake was hiring Dwight Clark to pick the best players for his newest franchise. Clark was famous for being on the other end of "The Catch" that saw Joe Montana find him in the corner of the endzone to defeat the Dallas Cowboys in the 1982 NFC Championship game. Clark finished the game with eight receptions for 120 yards and two touchdowns, but none bigger than that one snatch to win it.

After nine seasons playing with the 49ers, Clark retired following the 1987 season, and went on to work in their front office for the next decade. Clark was a part of three more Super Bowl runs through 1998 with the 49ers, and should have had an excellent eye for picking out talent. Again, sadly, he didn't.

Clark was hired by Policy, Lerner, and the Browns to become their first executive vice president and director of football operations. He would fail miserably and depart Cleveland by May 2002, when new head coach Butch Davis took over personnel decisions after being with the Browns just one season.

Speaking of Butch Davis, many fans incorrectly remember him as being the first head coach of the new Browns, but the first coach was actually Chris Palmer.

Palmer had a football odyssey in the coaching ranks before he ever set foot in Cleveland. He began his professional coaching career in 1983, when he was the offensive line coach for the Montreal Concordes in the Canadian Football League. The following year, he coached the wide receivers for the USFL's New Jersey Generals. In 1985, he was promoted to quarterbacks coach and offensive coordinator. It proved to be a great move for Palmer and the Generals as that was the same year that Herschel Walker ran for 2,411 yards. For Palmer, however, it would not last as the league folded shortly after.

Palmer's next stop would be in the college ranks as the head coach of Division II school New Haven. He would then spend two years with Boston University as their head coach, going a paltry 4–7 each year, before getting fired after two seasons with an 8–14 record.

From there, he spent time with the Houston Oilers, helping create the run-and-shoot offense. He was with New England as the quarterback coach when Drew Bledsoe took the Patriots to the Super Bowl, and with Jacksonville as they began to turn the corner into one of the AFC's better teams.

His résumé as a coach was improving, but he was still far from the first choice for the Browns. Cleveland badly wanted to hire red-hot Minnesota Vikings OC Bill Billick who was fresh off a tremendous 15–1 year as offensive coordinator of the Vikings. Minnesota was being heralded as the best team in the league and had it not been for a last-second field goal by Morten Anderson of the Atlanta Falcons, they would have made it to the Super Bowl against the Denver Broncos.

Billick was also credited for the rebirth of Randall Cunningham that season as he took the once-forgotten phenom and saw Cunningham toss thirty-four touchdown passes and 3,704 yards. The Vikings went 14–1 in the regular season with Cunningham at the helm as Billick pushed all the right buttons. The Browns wanted him badly, but Modell would burn the Brownies again as Billick chose Baltimore instead.

After their next four choices all said no, the Browns settled for Chris Palmer. In the two years running the show in Cleveland, Palmer's Browns went 5–27. Franchise quarterback Tim Couch was sacked a ridiculous 66 times in just 21 games in Palmer's system. Couch never had a chance, as he was hurt week 7 of the 2000 season and Palmer never coached him again after that.

The first draft pick for the Cleveland Browns in the 1999 expansion draft was Jim Pyne from the Detroit Lions. Pyne would go on to play two years at guard with the Browns and do very well during that stretch. He was elected team captain while with the Browns. He was named three times to *Muscle and Fitness*'s NFL all-strength team. With his blue collar work ethic complete with goatee and shaved head, he looked tough and played the part.

Perhaps the craziest thing about that expansion draft is that Pyne was only one of two players out of the thirty-seven selected by the Cleveland Browns to make any contribution to the team. The only other player selected in that draft that did anything at all was Tarek Saleh, who clogged a few holes in the middle of the defense.

Here is a full list of everyone the Browns selected in their expansion draft.

1. C. Jim Pyne, Detroit

2. D. E. Hurvin McCormack, Dallas

3. T. Scott Rehberg, New England

4. W. R. Damon Gibson, Cincinnati

5. C. Steve Gordon, San Francisco

6. L. B. Tarek Saleh, Carolina

7. G. Jeff Buckey, Miami

8. L. B. Jason Kyle, Seattle

9. D. E. Rod Manuel, Pittsburgh

10. L. B. Lenoy Jones, Tennessee

11. C. B. Tim McTyer, Philadelphia

12. L. B. Elijah Alexander, Indianapolis

13. T. Pete Swanson, Kansas City

14. S. Gerome Williams, San Diego

15. S. Marlon Forbes, Chicago

16. W. R. Justin Armour, Denver

17. T. Paul Wiggins, Washington

18. S. Duane Butler, Minnesota

19. W. R. Fred Brock, Arizona

20. C. B. Kory Blackwell, N.Y. Giants

21. C. B. Kevin Devine, Jacksonville

22. C. B. Ray Jackson, Buffalo

23. G. Jim Bundren, N.Y. Jets

24. G. Ben Cavil, Baltimore

25. R. B. Michael Blair, Green Bay

26. D. T. Antonio Anderson, Dallas

27. G. Orlando Bobo, Minnesota

28. L. B. James Williams, San Francisco

29. Q. B. Scott Milanovich, Tampa Bay

30. S. Eric Stokes, Seattle

31. R. B. Ronald Moore, Miami

32. R. B. Clarence Williams, Buffalo

33. W. R. Freddie Solomon, Philadelphia

34. S. Brandon Sanders, N.Y. Giants

35. D. T. Mike Thompson, Cincinnati

36. R. B. Jerris McPhail, Detroit

37. C. B. Antonio Langham, San Francisco

Now, about Tim Couch. He was the first rookie draft pick of the Cleveland Browns, and the first of the entire NFL Rookie Class in 1999. The quarterback out of Kentucky was seen as the "chosen one" and the man to lead the Browns into the new generation and millennium.

It was a disputed pick, however, as many wanted running back Ricky Williams out of Texas. Williams fell all the way to five and the New Orleans Saints. When you look at the guys drafted after Couch that year, it is just insane how much talent went. Donovan McNabb went to to the Philadelphia Eagles where he had a fantastic career at quarterback.

Running back Edgerrin James out of Miami was selected by the Colts, where he tore it up for years. Tory Holt went sixth overall to St. Louis, where he appeared in two Super Bowls with Kurt Warner. Not to mention the seventh overall pick, Champ Bailey, who went on to play cornerback for Washington at a high level for many years.

The Browns felt comfortable with Couch, and took him over Donovan McNabb (two to Philly), Akili Smith (third to Cincy), Dante Culpepper, (eleven to Minnesota), and Cade McKnown (twelve to Bears). With the exception of McNabb, Couch seemed like the best available QB and they took him.

Couch was big, strong, and had an arm like a rocket. While at Kentucky, in only two years as their starting quarterback, he launched 73 touchdowns next to only 33 interceptions. He also threw for 8,159 yards during that stretch. He was first team All SEC in 1998 and the SEC Player of the Year in 1998 as well. After being a finalist in the Heisman voting, he was considered a favorite to be the first overall selection to the brand-new Cleveland Browns, although, as mentioned, many fans wanted the Heisman Trophy–winning Ricky Williams.

To back up and mentor Couch, the Browns brought in Ty Detmer. Detmer came into the NFL in 1992 as a backup to Brett Favre before departing for the Eagles in 1996 and the 49ers in 1998. He had learned from Favre and Steve Young and picked up some playing time in Philly in the middle. He had started nineteen games in that stretch while throwing twenty-six touchdowns. He seemed like he would be a serviceable quarterback for Couch to learn from.

The goal was for Detmer to play the majority, if not all, of the first season as the starting quarterback. That plan was quickly aborted three quarters into opening night against Pittsburgh. A packed house saw the Browns get completely destroyed against their rival as the hype of opening night for the franchise quickly turned into a nightmare. The Browns lost 43–0 and Detmer was yanked for Couch after starting 6 of 13 for 52 yards and one interception while getting sacked twice and achieving one first down. It couldn't have gone any worse.

Palmer pushed the panic button and they went to Couch who promptly threw an interception on his first pass attempt in the NFL. He would finish 0 for 3 on the night. The Browns had just lost their franchise opener to their bitter rival, and it was horrific. They were held to just two first downs the entire game.

Sadly, for Browns fans, it never got much better as the Browns would finish 2–14 on the season. The first win came on Halloween in New Orleans. It was special for Browns fans but also for wide receiver Kevin Johnson. Just one week prior it was Johnson who had guaranteed the Browns would defeat the St. Louis Rams. The Rams were the best team in the league under Kurt Warner, Marshal Faulk, Tory Holt, and led by Dick Vermeil, known as the fastest show on turf. They reminded Cleveland of that with a 34–3 beatdown of the Browns.

Johnson needed to make the game-winning catch to get the media off his back for the first time in a week. Also noteworthy in this game was the fact that Ricky Williams, who a lot of Browns wanted the team to use the overall number one pick on, fumbled three times throughout the contest, the last of which gave Cleveland a chance at the Hail Mary and, ultimately, the victory.

But Cleveland just seemed snake-bitten at times, a trend that would sadly follow them for years to come. There was no bigger example of this than in the story of veteran offensive lineman Orlando Brown. Brown was an offensive lineman for the original Browns, as he arrived in Cleveland in 1993 and stayed with the franchise through their move to Baltimore in 1996. He was popular while in Cleveland and earned the nickname Zeus. Malley's Chocolate actually named a chocolate bar after him, as he was a shining member in the community among the youth.

Zeus stood at 6-foot-7, 360 pounds, and was known as an energetic and intimidating player on the field but a gentle giant off of it. Browns fans were ecstatic when he returned to Cleveland in 1999 after spending three years in Baltimore. Brown was one of only two players to have played for the original Cleveland Browns *and* the revived Browns, as most of the Browns roster was moved to Baltimore. The other player was Antonio Langham.

The fate of Zeus in his return to Cleveland was not a good one. On December 19, 1999, against the Jacksonville Jaguars, Brown was hit in the right eye by a penalty flag weighted with ball bearings thrown by referee Jeff Triplette. Triplette immediately apologized to Brown. Brown left the game temporarily, then returned to the field only to shove Triplette, knocking him to the ground. Brown was ejected from the game and had to be escorted off the field by his teammates. Brown was subsequently suspended by the NFL, but the suspension was lifted when the severity of his injury became apparent. Brown missed three seasons due to temporary blindness.

Brown sat out the entire 2000 NFL season waiting for his right eye to heal. The Browns released him after the season. In 2001, he sued the NFL for $200 million in damages. According to reports, he settled for a sum between $15 million and $25 million in 2002. It was just one of many stories of early struggle in Cleveland's return to the league.

Despite the horrendous and rushed first season that saw them lose eleven times by eleven or more points, Browns fans were still deliriously happy about the NFL being back in their city. The team was the youngest in football and it seemed as though they could only go up. It was the first time a team only won two games but the city was ecstatic. It wouldn't last.

Franchise quarterback Tim Couch started 14 games, throwing for 2443 yards and 15 touchdowns with 13 interceptions. Pretty low numbers, but not terrible considering he had next to no protection on the line and few targets to throw the ball to. He also had a lack of a running game considering their top rusher was Terry Kirby with only 452 yards and 6 touchdowns. Kirby did most of his damage catching dump-off passes and screens, finishing with 528 yards on 58 catches.

Browns fans loved to compare anyone they could to their favorites from the Bernie era of the 1980s and this bunch was no different. Their version of fan favorite Brian Brennan was rookie Darren Chiaverini. The slot receiver had 44 catches for 497 yards and 4 touchdowns. He didn't have a shred of the Brian Brennan talent, but he was a white slot receiver with decent hands, so fans clung to hope.

The new Webster Slaughter was fellow rookie and second round pick, Kevin Johnson. He was the thirty-second overall pick and third overall receiver picked in the 1999 NFL Draft. Big things were expected of Johnson and his rookie season gave fans some hope. He showed flashes of being a number-one receiver as he finished with a team high in catches and yards with 66 grabs for 986 yards and 8 touchdowns. The Johnson and Couch combination was supposed to be the new big thing in Cleveland.

The offensive struggles and lack of running game was one thing, but the Browns set their sights on defense as they entered the 2000 NFL Draft with the number one overall pick yet again. In 1999, they allowed 30 or more points 6 times, and 20 or more points 4 times. They couldn't stop the run, pressure the quarterback, or get off the field on third down.

The answer to increasing the pass rush, stopping the run, and solidifying the line was Courtney "The Quiet Storm" Brown, out of Penn State. Courtney Brown was one of the most physically dominant linemen to ever come out of the Big 10. He was a can't-miss prospect that no one questioned going number one overall. Brown was a Heisman Trophy candidate as a Nittany Lion and extremely coachable. He was also disciplined and Browns brass never had to worry about him getting into trouble off the field.

At 6 foot 4 inches, 285 pounds, and quick as a cat, Browns fans had visions of Brown one day wearing a gold jacket in Canton. There was only one small problem: he couldn't stay healthy. Brown would be out of the NFL by 2005 and miss thirty-six games throughout his career.

To make matters worse was some of the talent the Browns passed up to select Courtney Brown with the first overall pick. They passed up on LaVar Arrington (Washington), Chris Samuels (Washington), Jamal Lewis (Baltimore), Plaxico Burress (Pittsburgh), Brian Urlacher (Chicago), Julian Peterson (San Francisco), and Shaun Alexander (Seattle), just to name a few.

With Brown selected in the first round, the Browns continued to try and replicate their wide receivers of the 1980s with their second round pick of Dennis Northcutt. With his small size but lightning-quick speed, Northcutt resembled Gerald "The Ice Cube" McNeil. Like the Ice Cube, Northcutt could also return kicks.

At first, it looked as though the moves were starting to pay off and growth was happening as the Browns started the season 2–1 under Chris Palmer. After a week one 27–7 setback at home to the Jacksonville Jaguars, they rattled off two straight divisional wins over the Bengals and Steelers. They beat the Bengals in a 24–7 laugher on the road and then the Steelers in thrilling fashion at home, 23–20. You can say what you want about Palmer and Couch, but to this point, Couch was 2–0 as a starter against Pittsburgh and Palmer was 2–1 as a coach against Pittsburgh.

Things were looking promising, and then the wheels proceeded to fall off the cart. Over the final 13 weeks of the season, they were shut out 4 times, held to only 3 points 2 more times, and held under 10 points, 10 times total before the season was over. After getting blasted by Oakland 36–10 week 4 and getting shut out by the Ravens 12–0 week 5, things officially came to a crashing end week 6 when Tim Couch got hurt against Denver and never returned. Couch threw three picks in that game, got sacked 5 times, and broke his thumb, ending his season for good.

The Browns finished the season 3–13 and showed zero improvement without Couch in the lineup the final 10 weeks. They showed no fight for the coach, and this was never more evident than in weeks 13 and 14 in which they combined to lose to division rivals Baltimore and Jacksonville, 92 – 7.

Unlike after 1999 when the team had that new car feel and plenty of optimism to go around, this felt like a total dumpster fire. The franchise quarterback was banged up and never protected. There was no running game as your leading rusher was the scat back Travis Prentice with 512 yards. Backup quarterback Doug Pederson couldn't throw the ball more then 6 yards, and finished with 2 touchdowns and 8 interceptions. He only compiled 1,047 yards on 117 of 210 passing for a dismal 4.9 yards per attempt. Nothing went right.

Only two seasons in, the Browns had hit rock bottom. Any thought of playing to save Palmer's job was also tossed out with a pitiful 24–0 loss at home to Tennessee to end the season. Palmer would be gone days later and the Browns were looking at their first of many re-starts.

# CHAPTER 2

# Trusting Coach Butch

DAYS AFTER THE UNIVERSITY OF MIAMI HURRICANES WON THE 2001 Sugar Bowl with a decisive 37–20 victory over Florida, head coach Butch Davis said he would never leave the program as head coach and loved it in South Beach. Two weeks later he was the head coach of the Cleveland Browns.

Davis was regarded as the hottest commodity in coaching. His Hurricanes were seen as the best team in college football that year and it was a crime they didn't play in the National Championship Game. They went 11–1 and knocked off the #1 ranked Florida State Seminoles in week 5 with a 27–24 thrilling win at home. A few weeks later, they defeated the #2 ranked Virginia Tech Hokies and Michael Vick, 41–21 at home. The Canes had all the swagger of the nation's top team. The fact that the BCS chose Florida State to play Oklahoma in the championship game, which they would lose, 13–2, was a joke.

Davis arrived in Miami as the head coach of the Hurricanes in 1995, taking over a program that was facing serious sanctions from the Dennis Erickson era. Erickson had led them to a National Championship with Warren Sapp as well as Dwayne "The Rock" Johnson. Despite the sanctions, Davis met with instant success and led Miami to an 8–3 record and a share of the Big East championship. They repeated that the next season going 9–3. After a disastrous 1997 season that saw them go 5–6, the bounced back with nine wins again, in 1998 and 1999.

Perhaps the most impressive fact about Davis was his team's ability to win in the postseason. With the Hurricanes, he went 4–0 in bowl games.

It could have been 5–0, but the sanctions kept them out of the postseason the first year he was there. Davis was seen as a winner, and the Browns wanted and needed him badly.

Winning was nothing new to Davis, however, as he had been doing it since high school. He played for the Bixby Spartans out of Oklahoma where he was an all-state fullback and defensive end for the football team. After graduating in 1970, he attended the University of Arkansas and played defensive end for the Razorbacks. That is where his on-field career ended, as he injured his knee, required surgery, and never played again.

With one door closed, Davis walked through the coach's door and never looked back. He became a student assistant for the rest of his college career. After graduation from college, he held assistant coaching positions at Fayetteville High School in 1973, Pawhuska High School from 1974 to 1975, and Charles Page High School in Sand Springs, Oklahoma, from 1976 to 1977. He held his first head coaching job at Will Rogers High School in 1978. David was starting to develop a serious taste for coaching that would eventually lead him to become a part of the Dallas Cowboys dynasty.

For Davis, it started in 1979 when he met Jimmy Johnson and began a decade and a half partnership. He started first as a receivers and tight ends coach with the Oklahoma State University Cowboys under Johnson, then later as defensive line coach at the University of Miami. During their time in Miami, they won the 1987 NCAA National Championship.

When Johnson left "The U" to coach in the NFL with the Dallas Cowboys in 1989, he brought Davis with him. Davis began as the defensive line coach and eventually ascended to defensive coordinator. While Johnson and Davis were with the Cowboys, they won two NFL Super Bowls against the Buffalo Bills. After Johnson left, Davis spent a short time under Barry Switzer before leaving to coach at Miami.

Davis arrived in Cleveland when Browns fans and players were desperate for a leader. They needed a voice, someone to lead them, and that was Davis to a tee. While Chris Palmer had little respect from the locker room, Davis would change all of that—and quickly.

The Browns defense had been hideous under Palmer, and Davis was seen as a defensive mastermind. The change worked, as the Browns led the NFL in interceptions in 2001 with thirty-three. Davis led them to a 7–9 record, including two wins over the defending Super Bowl champion Baltimore Ravens.

The thing about Davis was that he not only commanded respect, but he was quickly given it. He wanted full control over the roster and was granted it by Lerner and Policy which led to Dwight Clark stepping down and leaving the team.

Davis preached defense and used his first draft pick, and the third overall pick in the 2001 NFL draft, on defensive tackle Gerard Warren. It was a good pick as he started 15 games his rookie season and finished with 61 tackles and 5 sacks. The pick didn't come without second guessing, however, as the Browns passed up future NFL MVP running back LaDainian Tomlinson out of TCU. The Browns still had no running game, and LT would go on to put up Hall of Fame numbers in his career.

The selection of Warren was the beginning of a trend for Davis as president and GM. He would consistently pick Florida-based players. Later in the 2001 draft he selected Miami running back James Jackson in the third round. In the fourth round he picked cornerback Anthony Henry out of South Florida. In the seventh round he picked up Andre King, a wideout out of Miami.

As mentioned, the Browns defense was much improved in 2001, and at least partially because of this draft. Warren helped solidify the line and the Browns showed dramatic results as the secondary had a much improved chance to lockdown the wideouts. This also gave the linebackers a much better shot at getting to the opposing quarterback, which they did. Linebacker Jamir Miller led the team with thirteen sacks and became the first Cleveland Brown to make the Pro Bowl since their return to the NFL.

Courtney Brown only played in 5 games because of injury, but managed 4.5 sacks in just 5 games. It only makes you wonder what his career could have been had he stayed healthy. Tyrone Rogers had 6 sacks while Greg Spires had 4. They still couldn't stop the run, but at the very least, they found the quarterback.

All of this pressure on the quarterback allowed the DBs to feast. Taking the most advantage was rookie Anthony Henry with 10 picks, including 3 in week 2 against Detroit. That was a game in which the Browns picked off Ty Detmer 7 times before it was over. Veteran safety Earl Little had 5 interceptions throughout the season while Daylon McCutcheon had 4. Corey Fuller and Raymond Jackson had 3 each as the team finished with the league high, 33.

The defense needed to step up as once again, the offense seemed to be stuck in the mud. Tim Couch showed little to no signs of improvement as he finished with just 17 touchdowns, next to 21 interceptions on 272 of 454 passing for 3,040 yards. While the numbers remained shaky for Couch, he had no one pushing for his job or even challenging, as he started all 16 games. His main target was once again Kevin Johnson who finished with 1,097 yards on 84 catches while scoring 9 times.

Part of the problem for Couch, besides the usual lack of protection, was also the lack of a number two threat he could rely on when Johnson was tightly covered. Rookie Quincy Morgan, the third in a long line for consecutive second round picks at wideout, finished with a paltry 30 catches for 432 yards. He was targeted 72 times, but had a serious case of the stone hands which led to countless drops.

For reasons unknown, fans seemed to love tight end Aaron Shea from Michigan. Shea only caught fourteen balls for eighty-six yards, but seemed to get the loudest roar every time he touched the ball.

How about the previous year's second-round draft pick, Dennis Northcutt? He didn't exactly make the jump they were hoping for, as he concluded the season with only 18 catches for 255 yards. Due to injuries, Northcutt would only start in 7 games and play in 11.

For the third straight season the Browns failed to produce a 1,000-yard rusher. Neither of their top two backs even came close. James Jackson compiled 554 yards on 195 carries with 2 touchdowns. The back that did show serious promise was Jamel White, who had 443 yards on the ground but also caught 44 balls for 418 yards in the air. Combined, White went for nearly1,000 yards of production with 6 touchdowns. Good for a fantasy team, but the Browns needed someone to win games with.

All of this being said, the team actually had a tremendous season of improvement and once again gave fans reason to hope. After losing their opener at home, 9–6 on a walk off field goal to Seattle, they bounced back in a big way. Cleveland would go on to win four of their next five games with a road win at Jacksonville, along with home wins against San Diego, Baltimore, and Jacksonville. The last two were huge wins because they came against good teams in the division. All of this was wrapped around a loss in Cincy that left them at 4–2 after six weeks.

At 4–2, things seemed almost too good to be true—and then they would quickly come crashing back down to earth. In the following game against the Chicago Bears, Couch had a touchdown pass to Johnson and Courtney Brown also had a 25-yard fumble return for a touchdown to lead 21–7. 5–2 looked like a sure thing with thirty seconds to go and the fourteen-point lead. The only thing that could stop them was a miracle comeback by Chicago, and what were the odds of that?

Apparently, much stronger than anyone realized as the Bears went on to make magic happen. A 9-yard touchdown pass from Shane Matthews to Marty Booker made it 21–14 with 28 seconds to go. Chicago would then recover the onside kick and convert a 34-yard Hail Mary to James Allen to tie the game at 21 with zero time remaining. The Browns would get the ball second in overtime, but it proved to be futile as a Tim Couch pass was picked off and returned sixteen yards for a clinching Bears touchdown by Mike Brown to complete the miracle comeback. This handed the Browns their third loss of the season.

As heartbreaking as that loss was, it would get even harder the following week at home. The Browns squandered a late 12–9 lead to arch rival Pittsburgh, losing 15–12 in overtime for the second straight week. Making matters even worse, it was their second loss of the year in which they didn't let up a single touchdown, but all field goals as Steeler kicker Kris Brown nailed five of them. The same thing had happened to them opening week against Seattle.

At 4–4, following back-to-back heartbreaking overtime losses, it would have been easy for the team to fold, but that is not who they were under Butch Davis. Instead of packing it in, they bounced back with two huge wins: A big road win at Baltimore and then an 18–0 shutout of

Cincinnati at home. They were suddenly two games over 500 and once again had a legitimate chance at the playoffs. In the win over the Bengals, Phil Dawson went 4 of 4 with field goals. He finished the season 22 of 25 as he was beginning to cement his place as one of the best kickers in Browns history.

Once again, the playoff dream would hit a serious roadblock as they proceeded to drop the next two games in ugly fashion. They lost back-to-back lopsided games to Tennessee and New England. The Patriots would go on to win the Super Bowl that season as the Tom Brady and Bill Belichick era was beginning.

Heading into week 12 against the Jaguars, at 6–6, they still had an outside chance at the playoffs but could not afford to lose any more games. Trailing 15–10 with a little over one minute to go in the game, Tim Couch began to lead what was a hopeful game-winning drive. As they began to advance the ball into Jaguar territory, they faced a fourth and two at the Jaguar twelve yard line, when Tim Couch looked to complete a pass over the middle to Quincy Morgan for the first down. It was a close call but ruled on the field as a narrow catch.

As the Browns ran to the line of scrimmage and quickly ran their next play, a Couch spike, the whistles began to blow shortly after the completion of the next play. Per the rule, once the ball had been snapped, the prior play couldn't be reviewed; however, lead official Terry McAulay claimed he was buzzed by the box before Couch snapped the ball, and thus, they were suddenly reviewing the Morgan catch. Confused yet? So was everyone watching at home, and the packed house at First Energy Stadium came unglued once the catch was overturned and the ball given back to Jacksonville.

Now, instead of watching Tim Couch lead a game-winning drive, Browns fans in the stadium were ducking for cover as the bottles began to fly. Browns fans began throwing objects onto the field, mainly beer bottles. A few especially irate fans began throwing the stadium's trash cans down to the field. After a few minutes of mayhem and constant arguing, the officials announced that the game would end forty-eight seconds early and the officials and players exited the field. It was unbelievable.

Some players reported getting hit, but none were seriously injured. A few fans ran onto the field, but were quickly apprehended by law enforcement. After a few minutes of waiting for the crowd to settle, the field had become littered with bottles and debris. Referee Terry McAulay, who blew the initial call and then called the game over, received a scathing call from the commissioner's office that he was wrong to stop the game and was forced to restart it.

Two kneel-downs later, and the Browns were 6–7 and out of playoff contention. The amazing part was later on in the press conference when Carmen Policy and Butch Davis both refused to put any blame on the fans, and all of it on the officials. This was despite the fact that countless fans were caught and barred from Browns game for life, and on top of that, one fan got nailed by a portable radio and was busted wide open.

The incident was so ugly that it resulted in a long overdue policy of limiting alcohol purchases to two drinks per person per concession stand visit, along with alcohol sales ending after the end of the third quarter. Bottles were no longer served with a lid, because a loaded bottle could do serious damage to a skull or face.

Speaking of ugly, this entire incident could have been avoided if Couch hit his man in stride, and Morgan actually knew how to hang onto the ball. It was the capper on a bad game for Couch that saw him get sacked three times and picked off once.

For Cleveland, they would lose two of their final three games to follow, dropping to 7–9 on the season. The one win came in Tennessee in week 15, when they came back from a 38–24 fourth quarter deficit to win 41–38 on a last-second field goal by Phil Dawson. Despite being out of the playoff chase, that win against the Titans meant a lot. It proved they would still play hard for coach Davis and showed their heart. This was a major difference from the prior season.

Despite being 7–9 and missing the playoffs for the third straight season, the Browns fans had plenty to be happy about. The team never lost its composure despite the rollercoaster season, a season that included the tragic 9/11 delay added into all of it. The defense was improved, the coach was well liked, and they still had that "franchise" quarterback who was going to start playing well consistently, any day now.

Heading into the 2001 offseason as the 2002 calendar year began, Browns fans had plenty of optimism. As the Browns prepared for the draft, they had quality veterans on the defense with Corey Fuller, Jamir Miller, Earl Little, and Dwayne Rudd. They then brought in several all-pros in the form of Kenard Lang, Robert Griffith, and Earl Holmes. All of this was mixed in with young former drafts picks of Daylon McCutcheon, Courtney Brown, and Gerard Warren.

They knew with all of that the defense could be counted on and it was the offense that had to be addressed with their first-round pick. They did just that by selecting William Green, a speedy and powerful running back out of Boston College with their first pick and the sixteenth overall pick. Then for the fourth straight season, took a wide receiver with their second round pick as they selected Andre Davis out of Virginia Tech.

Tim Couch reported to camp that summer bigger and stronger, and it appeared like he was finally going to turn the corner on his career. That lasted all of three preseason games until he hurt his arm and missed the first two games of the regular season.

It was difficult for Couch to have to sit out, but the one thing that kept him calm was the fact that he was never questioned as the starting quarterback, and no one even challenged him for his spot. He was the chosen one, and that was all there was to it. Well, all of that changed week one as Kelly Holcomb went off against the Kansas City Chiefs in a narrow 40–39 shootout loss. Holcomb threw for 326 yards and three touchdowns. It was the kind of performance Browns fans had been expecting and not getting from Couch for three seasons.

The Browns would have won the game, had it not been for an extremely bizarre turn of events with zero time remaining on the clock. A last second field goal attempt was blocked and as a linebacker whipped off his helmet in full celebration mode, the Chiefs recovered and advanced the ball. Because the play was still live when he took his helmet off, the refs threw the flag, and bottle gate was now replaced with helmet gate as the Browns' most painful loss in their newest regime. Sadly, and without question, Chiefs placekicker and NFL Hall of Famer Morten Anderson nailed the thirty-yard field goal on the next play for the most recent in a seriesof opening week losses for Cleveland.

Holcomb led them to victory the next week, with a convincing 20–7 win over Cincinnati which saw him through for 198 yards and two more touchdowns next to zero interceptions. Holcomb was a beast, and exactly what this team needed. Kevin Johnson was also playing well with Holcomb, as he had 15 catches and nearly 200 yards in the first two weeks.

But, if you're Coach Davis, how do you not go back to your overall first pick in Tim Couch when he is ready? He had no choice, and did exactly that as they entered week three on the road in Tennessee. It's hard to blame Davis—heading into 2002, Holcomb had been in the NFL in 1997 with the Colts, where he threw seventy-three passes, and then out of the league until becoming Couch's backup the year prior. Either he was becoming the greatest Cinderella story of all time, or this was some sort of fluke.

Davis rolled the dice and went back to his "franchise quarterback" in Couch. At first it looked like a giant mistake, as the Browns trailed Tennessee 28–14 with just three minutes left in the game. Couch then did what Couch did best and ledgame-winning and tying drives. The Browns rallied under Couch to score two touchdowns in the final 2:35 to send the game to overtime. The scores came on the arm of Couch as he hooked up with Andre Davis and Dennis Northcutt. Phil Dawson would put it away for good in overtime with a thirty-three-yard field goal.

Couch bounced back from some early rust and had a monster game with 326 yards and three touchdowns. It was the exact same stat line Holcomb had week one, and it appeared as though Couch was up for the challenge. Sadly, for Tim and the Browns, it was anything but the following two weeks.

The Browns lost their next game to Pittsburgh, once again in overtime, 16–13 as Steelers' backup quarterback and XFL MVP Tommy Maddox came in to defeat them. As painful as that loss was, it became even wilder the following week as the Browns welcomed the Baltimore Ravens to town for Sunday Night Football. It was an emotional night as Al Lerner had just passed away from brain cancer earlier in the week and the Browns crowd was louder than ever before. They wanted this one for Al!

Through three quarters on national television, the Browns were getting embarrassed by their bitter rival 23–0 in a shellacking. Tim Couch was playing awfully, tossing two interceptions and seemingly lost before finally reaching the endzone to begin the fourth quarter. He connected with Mark Campbell for the score, and then found Morgan in the back of the endzone for a two-point conversion. Suddenly Couch was red hot and the Browns trailed 23–8 with 14:15 left in the game.

When the Browns got the ball back, Couch got sacked and knocked out. When he came to, the crowd started cheering as Kelly Holcomb ran on the field. Couch, who was still groggy, simply heard the fans cheering and mistook it for them cheering his injury. He would sound off on it in the Browns locker room postgame as he started crying and expressed his concern with the fans. That was the beginning of the end for Couch in Cleveland.

Meanwhile the crowd went absolutely nuts as they witnessed Holcomb lead one hell of a comeback. Over the next ten minutes, Holcomb connected with Dennis Northcutt twice in the endzone to cut into the lead at 26–21 with over a minute to go. The Browns got the ball back one more time after a converted onside kick and once again moved inside of the Ravens ten-yard line. The Holcomb magic would finally run out as he was picked off to end the game. The Browns stadium went from the loudest it has ever been to pure silence when Ed Reed stepped in front of the Holcomb pass.

In just 10 minutes of action, Kelly Holcomb went for 180 yards on 13 of 23 passing with 2 touchdowns. How do you go away from that? Davis once again had a problem on his hands as they prepared to travel to Tampa Bay the next week. Once again, he stuck with Couch and they lost 17–3. Couch went 20 of 40 for 151 yards, no touchdowns, and 1 pick. The Buccaneers went on to win the Super Bowl that year on the strength of that incredible defense.

Davis continued to stick with Couch, and slowly it began to pay off as the Browns bounced back to defeat the expansion Houston Texans 34–17. The following week they traveled to New York where Couch led a second-half comeback to beat the Jets 24–21. They were once again at

500, 2–2, as they hosted the Steelers, in another three-point losing effort 23–20 to fall to 4–5 on the season.

While the 4–5 start was a letdown and very frustrating for Cleveland, it wasn't anything compared to the letdown of first round pick William Green. Through 9 games, he had lost his starting job to journeyman Jamel White. Green was a disaster as he was held to an abysmal 161 yards on 71 carries. This was insanely low, averaging out to 17 yards a game on an average of 2.2 yards per carry. He was held to 2 yards against Baltimore, 8 yards against the Jets and 10 against Pittsburgh. Through 9 games, he looked like the biggest running back bust in NFL draft history.

Then, a strange thing happened: when Jamel White got hurt, Green stepped back into the starting role and took off! Over the final 7 games, Green busted out for 726 yards which averaged to over 100 yards a game. He'd finish the year with 887 yards as he went from total bust to permanent starter in perhaps one of the greatest single-season turnarounds of all time.

Green's incredible turnaround over the final seven games allowed the Browns to go on a 5–2 run and make the playoffs. This was highlighted with last-second come-from-behind wins over Jacksonville, Baltimore, and Atlanta along the way. The Jacksonville game saw a Hail Mary to end it from Couch to Morgan while the Falcon game was a must-win to make the playoffs that saw a Green sixty-four-yard touchdown run to cap it!

The Browns were 9–7 and headed to the playoffs for the first time in their new existence. There was only one small problem: the come-from-behind win over Atlanta to make the playoffs was not led by Tim Couch, but rather, Kelly Holcomb as Couch was knocked out of the game. Couch broke his fibula and was now done for the year. Browns fans had screamed for Holcomb all season long, and they were about to get him!

Couch had lackluster numbers on the season, finishing with 18 touchdowns and 18 interceptions in 14 starts. Despite several comeback wins, he simply wasn't the guy to lead the Browns. Holcomb may have been lightning in a bottle, but he was showing up at the perfect time as a playoff matchup in Pittsburgh awaited them.

Following two losses by 3 points each, the Browns felt they were dead even compared to the 10–5–1 Steelers. The Steelers actually started the year 0–2 with Kordell Stewart as their quarterback before having an oddly timed bye week 3. Maddox would come in to replace Stewart week 4 against the Browns and lead them to victory. Under Maddox, they went 10–3–1, not bad at all for a guy who had been taking snaps for the LA Xtreme of the XFL just one year prior.

Still, the Browns had a running back who was tearing up the league to complete the regular season, a quarterback who seemed to find the endzone every time he touched the ball, and a veteran defense that was more than ready for the moment.

Through three and a half quarters into the snowy day in Pittsburgh on January 5, 2003, everything looked to be going Cleveland's way. The Browns led 33–21 with five minutes to go and northeast Ohio football fans were experiencing an orgasmic football frenzy as their beloved Ohio State Buckeyes had won the National Championship just thirty-six hours earlier over Miami, and now their Brownies were about to knock the hated Steelers out of the playoffs on their home turf. Sadly, it all changed in a heartbeat.

Maddox would find patented Browns killer Hines Ward to cut into the lead 33–28 with 3:06 left to play. The Browns still had a chance to win, however, as all they needed to do was run out the clock. It looked as though they would do exactly that as Holcomb hit Dennis Northcutt right in the hands on a third down toss that should have iced the game. Northcutt dropped it and the Browns had to punt. The veteran laden defense of the Browns finally gave out, as Maddox led a game-winning drive to send Cleveland home 36–33.

It was the third loss to Pittsburgh that season, all by three points. This one was by far the most painful as Kelly Holcomb once again played incredibly well, finishing with 429 yards and 3 touchdowns on 26 of 43 passing. What more could he have done? Cleveland was in love with Holcomb and the Browns brass would have a major decision on their hands that offseason.

Coach Davis and the Browns would eventually go with their "gut" and name Kelly Holcomb to start behind center the next season after a mini QB battle in training camp and preseason. The highlight of that battle saw a packed house go bananas during a preseason game against the visiting Green Bay Packers as Holcomb and Couch both exchanged touchdown passes in a first-class shootout. The fans in the stands for that preseason game were actually the only ones to physically see it, however, as most of Northeast, Ohio, was without electricity during a record long blackout in the summer of 2003.

Things didn't go as many thought they would, however. After lighting up the league every time he played in 2002, Holcomb was flat to start the season and the Browns stumbled out of the gate to a 1–2 record. In their one win, Holcomb led them back from being down 12–0 in the fourth quarter on the road against powerhouse San Francisco. Holcomb launched two touchdown passes in the closing minutes to Andre Davis to win the game and avoid the 0–3 start. What was even more incredible is that he did this while playing with a broken fibula—the exact same injury Couch got the year before that allowed Holcomb to play in the playoff game.

From there, Couch would start the next five games as the Browns struggled to a 2–3 record during that stretch. Despite knocking off the defending AFC Champion Oakland Raiders and also the Steelers in Pittsburgh, Couch looked miserable once again and his play prohibited them from winning. Holcomb actually came off the bench in their losses to San Diego and New England, and both times almost sparked a comeback win.

The one memorable game during that entire ordeal was the blowout of Pittsburgh on Sunday Night Football. It was the last time the Browns won a regular season game in the Steel City. Remember now, this was October of 2003. It's just heartbreaking the dominance Pittsburgh has had at Heinz Field ever since.

They would eventually fall to 3–6 and cut Kevin Johnson from the team for lack of production and attitude issues. At first, it seemed like a smart move as they went out and destroyed Arizona 44–6 the following week, a game in which Holcomb threw for 392 yards and 3 touchdowns. The touchdowns were to Andre Davis, Quincy Morgan, and Dennis Northcutt.

Perhaps with the negative attitudes of Tim Couch on the bench and Kevin Johnson in free agency, the 4–6 Browns would finally turn it around? It was false hope as they finished the year 5–11. Holcomb got hurt on a Monday night against St. Louis, and that was pretty much it.

As bad as the post playoff season turned out to be, perhaps the most shocking was the off-the-field issues of William Green. After a good start with 559 yards in seven games, Green was arrested for drunk driving and marijuana possession. While on suspension from the NFL for that mishap, he got into a domestic violence issue with his girlfriend and was stabbed in the back. He would miss the final nine games of the horrendous season and was never the same.

For all the hype of the big battle between Kelly Holcomb and Tim Couch, ironically, because of Kelly Holcomb's injuries, they both ended up starting 8 games each. Neither exactly lit it up as Holcomb finished with 10 touchdown passes and 12 interceptions while Couch put up 7 touchdowns next to 6 interceptions.

The offseason was wild as it saw the departure of Tim Couch and the arrival of NFL All-Pro quarterback Jeff Garcia. It would do little to turn around the Browns' luck as they finished the 2004 season 4–12 and suffered a 9-game losing streak during it.

As for Coach Davis, in what can only be described as irony, in his last game as head coach of the Browns he elected to start Kelly Holcomb who promptly went out and tossed 5 touchdown passes while compiling 413 yards in a 58–48 wild loss at Cincinnati. Davis left midway through the 2004 season, and yet again, as 2005 was set to begin, so was another Browns reboot.

CHAPTER 3

# The Soldier, the Wolverine, and Camp Romeo

WHILE THIS BOOK IS ABOUT THE PLAYOFF YEARS, THERE IS ONE non-playoff year in the new Browns regime that stands out as one of the most fun for fans and what almost looked like a total dynasty to come. Sadly, it was not to be, but for fans, the 2007 season of Cleveland Browns football was simply a taste and teaser of just how fun things could be when the team went 10–6 and became one of the few teams in NFL history to win ten games yet narrowly miss the playoffs.

It all started with the 2004 NFL Draft when Butch Davis was still running the show regarding Cleveland Browns personnel. The Browns saw franchise quarterbacks Eli Manning and Phillip Rivers along with cannot-miss wideout Larry Fitzgerald and lights out safety Sean Taylor come off the board by the time they picked at six. Despite four studs already off the board, it was okay, because "The Soldier" had landed in their lap—University of Miami tight end Kellen Winslow was sitting there for the taking.

It didn't matter that Ohio-born Big Ben Roethlisberger was the pro-totypical quarterback of their dreams, and sitting right there, they went with their soldier! The Browns had acquired Jeff Garcia in the offseason, and Davis was ready to hitch his wagon to him for better or worse.

The fans loved the pick of Winslow, the media loved the pick, and the team loved the pick. He was the top threat coming out and seen as an instant game changer. Northeast Ohio fans knew him well from the 2003

National Championship game against their beloved Ohio State Buckeyes where Winslow caught eleven balls for 122 yards and a touchdown. He was the top receiver in a game that also saw first rounds studs Andrew Johnson, Roscoe Parrish, Michael Jenkins, and Chris Gamble all catch balls.

In two seasons as a starter with the Hurricanes, Winslow caught 117 balls for 9 touchdowns and 1,331 yards. His freshman year he appeared in 10 games, but these stats simply reflect his sophomore and junior seasons. He won the John Mackey Award as the nation's best collegiate tight end, and he was recognized as a unanimous first-team All-American, after receiving first-team honors from the Associated Press and other national selector organizations.

The "Soldier" nickname came from a game against the Tennessee Volunteers. The eighteenth-ranked Tennessee Vols defeated #6 Miami on the Hurricanes' home field by a score of 10–6. After a sweep play that saw Winslow take out two Volunteers to make way for Devin Hester, he got up screaming and taunting in typical "U" fashion. When questioned about the play afterward, he replied with "I'm a fucking soldier!"

This was despite the fact he never served in the military and the United States was in the middle of a war in Afghanistan. Not to mention the fact that he was unconcerned with the fact that his team had lost a major game, costing them a chance at the National Championship. He was simply about himself and making it known, he was a soldier.

None of that mattered to Butch Davis and the Cleveland Browns. They needed a scoring threat, and he was a serious one! He was the highest-selected tight end in more than thirty years. Davis was also well familiar with Winslow as it was he who recruited Winslow to the University of Miami before leaving for Cleveland in 2001. Almost instantly, there were issues as he was a contract holdout, demanding more money until Cleveland finally caved and gave him a six-year $40 million deal, including a $16.5 million signing bonus.

Perhaps most appealing about Winslow was that his father Kellen Sr. was an NFL legend with the San Diego Chargers and current NFL Hall of Famer. He was very well respected and it almost seemed like a sure thing that Winslow Jr. would follow in his father's footsteps. But it simply wasn't meant to be.

Winslow lasted all of two games into his rookie season before being lost for the year. In two games, he was held to 5 catches for 50 yards and was a total non-factor. In typical Browns fashion, he got hurt on an onside kick attempt in the closing moments of their 19–12 loss to Vinny Testaverde and the Dallas Cowboys. Why he was even in the game is anyone's guess, but just like that, all that hype was over for the season.

As mentioned earlier, Davis wouldn't make it through the rest of the 2004 season, and interim head coach Terry Robiskie took over after week 11. The team finished 4–12 during a horrendous season.

Randy Lerner had taken over the Browns for his father after Al Lerner passed in October of 2002. The long list of mistakes in hirings from the younger Lerner began with his hire of Romeo Crennel to take over as head coach in Cleveland. Crennel had been the defensive coordinator for the Browns during the abysmal 2000 season but was sent packing when Butch Davis arrived in the winter of 2001.

Coach Romeo was lovable and the kind of guy you wanted to play for. He wasn't feared like Davis was, but he seemed to have a nature that players, fans, and media would love, with a giant smile on his face. He, like Winslow, also had a winning pedigree. Unlike Kellen, his winning experience was self-made and not inherited. Romeo was on the staff of the Giants under Bill Parcells when they won the Super Bowl in 1987 and 1991. This was after ten years of coaching at Western Kentucky, Texas Tech, Ole Miss, and Georgia Tech.

Being with big-name programs and coaching in huge games was what Crennel was all about. He would then follow Parcells to his coaching stints with the Patriots and Jets where he was met with more winning as an assistant. Speaking of the Patriots and winning, after his disastrous season with Cleveland, Crennel joined another Parcells disciple, Bill Belichick, and was on his staff for three Super Bowl wins between 2001 and 2004.

Between coaching with Parcells and Belichick, the "Bills" had brought him five Super Bowl rings. Crennel came with clout, and a resume that couldn't be ignored. There was only one tiny, itsy-bitsy, super small problem: he had never been a head coach a day in his life, let alone at the NFL level. The inexperience would show quickly as the Browns stumbled to a 4–7 start to the season.

At 4–7, one thing was apparent: veteran journeyman quarterback Trent Dilfer, whom they brought in to start the year, wasn't the answer. Dilfer started eight games for the 2001 Baltimore Ravens where he wasn't asked to do much more than hand the ball off to Jamal Lewis and Priest Holmes while one of the best defenses in NFL history won them the Super Bowl. Say what you want about Dilfer, but they went 7–1 with him under center that season, including the playoff run.

Through his 11 games in Cleveland, Dilfer was immobile and subpar. He was 199 of 333 passing with only 11 touchdowns and 12 interceptions. Like Garcia the year before, Dilfer was also without "The Soldier," as Winslow never made it to a single practice that season. After recovering from the injury he received during his rookie season, Winslow promptly hurt himself again.

On May 1, 2005, Winslow suffered another leg injury when he was thrown from his Suzuki GSX-R750 motorcycle while speeding and trespassing in the Tri-C Corporate College parking lot in Westlake, Ohio. It resulted in a torn anterior cruciate ligament in his right knee and he was placed on the "Physically Unable-to-Perform (Non Football Injury)" list for the 2005 season. The fun wasn't over yet however; his bad luck just kept coming. Winslow later had a six-week-long staph infection that resulted from the injury.

With the NFL journeyman quarterback Dilfer not exactly lighting the world on fire, and Winslow falling off his tricycle, Crennel turned to a couple of rookies in hopes of finishing the year strongly. The first was rookie quarterback and Willard, Ohio, product Charlie Frye. The Akron Zip was selected in the third round (67 overall) of the 2005 NFL Draft by the Browns. Frye broke fifty-four football records during his college career at the University of Akron and seemed to come with the Cleveland moxie.

Despite the fact he was the fourth selected quarterback overall in a very weak QB class, the Browns fans didn't care and looked at him as the savior. He was a local product and that erased any doubt in their eyes. He started off well as he helped the Browns finish 2–3 during that stretch to close out 2005. The two wins were come-from-behind victories over the Raiders and Ravens which instantly endeared him to Browns fans and helped them forget about the 41–0 drubbing they took at home to Pittsburgh during that stretch.

During that short sample size, he formed instant chemistry with fellow rookie Braylon Edwards out of Michigan. The Wolverine struggled to stay healthy, though, only starting 7 games because of injuries. He shined in those starts, catching 32 balls for 512 yards and 3 touchdowns. Not exactly world-beater numbers, but he showed flashes of brilliance if and when he could just hang on to the football. He had fleet feet but hands of stone.

Edwards came in with an extreme amount of hype and promise as he was another can't-miss product. Having him line up next to Kellen Winslow almost seemed too good to be true when they took him third overall. His numbers at Michigan were incredible as he grabbed 252 catches in four seasons with 3,541 yards and 39 touchdowns. He was seen as the best player in college football the 2004 season, and it wasn't even close.

During his senior season in 2004, he set Michigan season records for receptions (97) and receiving yards (1,330), and career records with 252 receptions, 3,541 yards, and 39 touchdowns, which was also a Big Ten record. Edwards also set the Michigan career record for the most games with 100 or more receiving yards and following his senior season, he won the Fred Biletnikoff Award given to the nation's top receiver. He was the Big Ten Conference's most valuable player, and was recognized as a unanimous first-team All-American.

Edwards is the only wide receiver in Big Ten history and the third in NCAA Division I-A annals to gain 1,000 or more receiving yards in three consecutive years. Not only that, but he was red hot coming into the draft as Edwards concluded his college career by recording three touchdown catches in the 2005 Rose Bowl against the Texas Longhorns, tying the Rose Bowl record. The Cleveland Browns were getting the next Jerry Rice, Steve Largent, and Randy Moss all in one. Despite a rough rookie season for Edwards, they knew they had a total stud at wideout.

To go along with the young nucleus at quarterback and wideout, the Browns finally seemed to have a solid running game as well with Reuben Droughns. The Browns had given up William Green coming into the 2005 season, and Coach Crennel was set on Droughns as his guy. It was a smart decision as Droughns used his five-foot 11-inch, 220-pound frame as a battering ram all season long. He could plow through the line, and he could also cut back and find holes.

He seemed to be the total package as he finished with 1,232 yards on 309 carries while also catching 39 balls for 369 yards. It also erased the common thought that he was the product of the Denver running system the year before when he went for 1,240 yards and 6 touchdowns with the Broncos. He very much appeared to be the real deal.

Hopes were high heading into 2006 as the name of the game for the Browns was consistency. They had Romeo Crennel coming back for year two at the helm. Both Braylon Edwards and Kellen Winslow were coming back to start the season healthy. Charlie Frye and Reuben Droughns were also both back and ready to lead the offense.

As for new additions, they signed all-pro punter Dave Zastudil who was from Bay Village, Ohio. He spent his first four seasons with the Ravens where he became one of the best punters in the league before signing with his hometown Browns.

Speaking of big-name hometown free agent signings, there was none bigger than LeCharles Bentley: He played his high school ball in Cleveland at Saint Ignatius and college ball in Columbus. He was a two-year starter in high school and a three-year letterman, earning All-Ohio honors as a senior in 1997 as a Wildcat. His career as an Ohio State Buckeye went every bit as well, where he was a four-year letterman for them from 1998 to 2001. As a senior in 2001, he won the Remington Trophy as college football's best center. He received first-team All-Big Ten Conference honors, and was recognized as a consensus first-team All-American.

He was drafted by the New Orleans Saints in 2002 and instantly took off. He was named *Sports Illustrated*'s Offensive Rookie of the Year in 2002 and Pro Football Weekly All-Rookie Team. In 2005, he started fourteen games at center and was voted to the Pro Bowl for the third straight season. The Saints tried to sign him long-term, but he wanted to be a Cleveland Brown badly and signed with them.

It was a huge coup for the Browns as he was regarded by ESPN as the top-rated free agent. They had now signed two of the top free agents simply because the men wanted to play for their hometown team. All the breaks seemed to be going their way.

They even picked up Kameron Wimbley, a tremendous pass rusher out of Florida State with the thirteenth pick in the NFL draft. As a senior, he recorded three multiple sack games and led the ACC in sacks. He also led the team in quarterback hurries with seventeen and set career-highs in season sacks and tackles for a loss. Despite being injured part of the season, Wimbley was named second team All-ACC and was named All-America by Pro Football Weekly.

The free agent frenzy for the Browns continued as on March 15, 2006, they signed Patriot All Pro linebacker Willie McGinest, reuniting with head coach Romeo Crennel, who was the Patriots' defensive coordinator during McGinest's stint in New England. McGinest signed a three-year deal worth $12 million with $6 million in guarantees and bonuses.

For the first time since the 2002 playoffs, it felt good to be a Browns fan. The enthusiasm and wishful thinking wouldn't last long, however. LeCharles Bentley tore his patellar tendon on the first play of the team's first 11-on-11 training camp session on July 27, and he missed the entire 2006 season. Because of a series of staph infections (yet again) to follow, he would never play again.

What hope was left seemed to go out the window on the very first play during the season opener. On the very first snap of the season, the Browns and Crennel were determined to show fans that things would finally be different. They ran a flea flicker that saw Reuben Droughns take the handoff and then pitch the ball back to Charlie Frye, who launched the ball 74 yards down the field to a wide open Braylon Edwards for a touchdown. First Energy Stadium went nuts as the winds of change seemed to be blowing and perhaps the football gods had decided to stop poking needles into the Browns voodoo doll. Just like the signing of Bentley, the excitement would be short-lived as the play was called back on a Kevin Shaffer holding penalty, and the Browns never recovered. Cleveland would go on to lose to the Saints 19–14 as Charlie Frye was up and down all game, finishing with three touchdowns and two interceptions.

The loss to the Saints was a sign of things to come, as the Browns would finish 4–12, and get blown out in 5 of their last 6 games. Charlie Frye didn't progress as they would have liked. The Zip finished with just 10 touchdown passes next to 17 interceptions in 13 starts. He missed 3 starts due to injury and his backup Derrick Anderson was even more dreadful. Anderson tossed 8 interceptions during that stretch.

Reuben Droughns fell back to earth as he started 12 games and only rushed for 758 yards. He would depart for the Giants in the offseason. While he may have fizzled, the combination of Kellen Winslow Jr. and Braylon Edwards took off as hoped. Edwards had 661 yards on 84 catches with 6 touchdowns while "The Soldier" had 89 catches for 879 yards and 3 touchdowns. The best stat for those two: they played all 16 games!

Perhaps Randy Lerner was too busy watching his Premier Club Aston Villa FC on the pitch to notice that his head coach Romeo Crennel had now gone 10–22 in two seasons at the helm. Not to mention the fact that Crennel would now be on his third offensive coordinator in three years as he went from Maurice Carthon to Jeff Davidson to Rob Chudzinski. It didn't matter, and the highly luxurious and low-maintenance "Camp Romeo" was open for year three.

Heading into 2007, little if anything was expected of the Browns, despite the fact that they had two top six picks catching the ball in Braylon Edwards and Kellen Winslow Jr. They still needed a left tackle to block for Charlie Frye, and someone, anyone, to hand the ball off to. They wasted no time addressing both issues early into the 2007 offseason.

Cleveland Browns GM Phil Savage looked like a genius the year prior with the free agent class he brought in, and he was about to do it again. With the hopes of Bentley returning long gone, they needed line help and got it. On March 3, 2007, the Browns signed former Cincinnati Bengals All Pro offensive guard Eric Steinbach to a seven-year contract. The team also signed former Miami Dolphins offensive guard Seth

McKinney to a one-year contract. It was also clear to Savage that Charlie Frye wasn't the answer, so they went after Trent Green from Kansas City, but couldn't nab him as he would be traded to the Miami Dolphins.

Savage wasn't done yet, however, as he still had the huge hole in the run game to fill and did so by taking a stud back away from the enemy. Jamal Lewis was drafted fifth overall by the Baltimore Ravens in the 2000 draft out of Tennessee and instantly took off. He ran for 1,364 yards in his rookie year, and then after missing his sophomore season with injury, came back to run for 1,327 yards in 2002.

In 2003, he was the top back in the game as he rushed for 2006 yards. It was just forty yards short of officially breaking the all-time single-season rushing record, which remains Eric Dickerson's 2,105 record-breaking yards in 1984. Earlier in 2003, on September 14, 2003, Lewis broke Corey Dillon's single-game rushing record of 278 yards by running for 295 yards against—you guessed it—the Cleveland Browns. He would go on to be NFL MVP in 2003.

He remained a top back in 2004, 2005 and 2006 as he rushed for 3,004 combined yards. The problem for Baltimore GM Ozzie Newsome was that Lewis's numbers were slipping a bit, and he had Mike Anderson chomping at the bit to play. They released Lewis and the Browns finally caught a rare inter-division break.

Even with the bump on the line from Steinbach, Savage knew the Browns needed a left tackle, and with a high pick in the draft, went out and got one by selecting Joe Thomas third overall. Thomas was as blue collar as they came, playing his college ball at Wisconsin and being out on a boat fishing when they picked him. Savage showed faith in Lewis with that pick as well, as he passed over dynamic running backs Marshawn Lynch and Adrian Peterson.

The selection of Thomas wasn't exactly a stretch. Thomas won the Outland Trophy as the nation's top interior lineman, and he was recognized as a consensus first-team All-American. No one disputed him as the top lineman in the country, and the Browns, like they did with Edwards a few years back, had the best player in the draft fall in their laps.

Then, the draft got interesting, very interesting, as Notre Dame quarterback and top prospect Brady Quinn began to slide. Almost every draft pundit had him going top five, and by the tenth pick, with him still on the board, ESPN and the NFL Network began to show him after every pick, becoming more and more frustrated.

Like Frye, Brady was another Ohio-born product, growing up in Columbus and playing his high school ball at Dublin Coffman. He tore it up at Notre Dame in 2005, averaging 110 more passing yards per game than he had as a sophomore while increasing his number of touchdown passes from 17 in 2004 to 32 in 2005. Quinn was named to the 2005 AP All-America Team as a third-team quarterback.

In 2006, he only got better. Quinn finished the season with 3,426 yards on 289 completions out of 467 attempts for a completion percentage of 61.9 percent and 7.34 yards per attempt. He threw 37 touchdowns to only 7 interceptions, and was sacked 31 times. Quinn finished the regular season with a passing efficiency rating of 146.65. Quinn won numerous awards, including the Johnny Unitas Golden Arm Award for the best college quarterback in the nation as well as the Maxwell Award for the best college football player. By the time he left Notre Dame, he had thrown for 11,762 yards and 95 touchdowns.

Once ESPN showed him taking a phone call after the twenty-first pick, Cleveland fans became excited and started to think wishfully. They didn't have another first round pick, but when the helmet switched from the Cowboys to the Browns, and a trade was announced, the Quinn frenzy took off. Many fans wanted the Browns to take Quinn at 3, so to get him at 22 and still get Thomas at 3 seemed like Nirvana!

In typical fashion, Quinn would become a holdout at camp, causing him to fall to third on the depth chart behind Derek Anderson and Charlie Frye coming into the season. Quinn eventually signed a five-year deal with the Browns worth a reported $20.2 million, with $7.5 million guaranteed and up to $30 million in incentives which allowed him to play and light it up in the third pre-season game.

Here the Browns went again to start the season with some hope, but not much. The countdown clock was on for Romeo to be fired, and Quinn to eventually start at quarterback at some point. After the week 1 drubbing at home to rival Pittsburgh in a 34–7 loss, it didn't seem like either would take long to occur. It mirrored the original home opener to Pittsburgh back in 99 when they lost 41–0.

Charlie Frye went 4 of 10 with 5 sacks and a pick before being benched in favor of Derek Anderson. Joe Thomas played his first and worst game as a pro with several false starts, holding calls and missed blocks. Little did we realize on that day, how incredible he would become, starting with that very season!

Phil Savage and the Browns front office wasted little time reacting, shipping Frye off to Seattle and promoting Anderson to full-time starter. The move was looked at as being temporary, and the actual plan was to have Quinn starting by week 8 in another rebuild of a season. Again, little did anyone realize just how good of a move the Anderson promotion would turn out to be.

Starting the very next week against Cincinnati where Anderson put up a 5-touchdown, 328-yard performance, the new starter would go on to have one of the greatest seasons in Cleveland Browns history. He was tremendous and led the Browns to 10 wins for the first time in decades, as he threw for 3,787 yards and 29 touchdowns. The only problem with Anderson seemed to be that the 19 interceptions he threw were almost always directly to the other team. It wasn't a case of tipped balls or bad routes; he was giving it right to the opposition.

Even with that said, it was easy to ignore because of the incredible success Anderson had. As mentioned, he helped the Browns take down the Bengals in a shootout 51–45 in one of the most high-scoring games in First Energy Stadium History. From there they rotated two home wins over Miami and Baltimore around two road losses to New England and Oakland to enter the bye week at 3–3.

It was still early into the season, but for the first time since 2002 the fans were still talking playoffs going into a bye week. They were right to do so as the Browns took off following the bye week with back-to-back wins over the Rams, and an overtime win over Seattle. The win over the Rams came on the road and saw them overcome an early 14–0 deficit. The win over Seattle was one of the most dramatic and loudest wins in First Energy Stadium history as well. It went into overtime, and was the first time that season that fans really started to buy in.

The 33–30 overtime win against Seattle brought on every emotion possible for Browns fans. They saw the Browns overcome a 21–6 hole, to battle back and take the lead 30–27 on a Lewis touchdown run with 2:17 to play. Seattle would hit a field goal as time ran out in regulation to send it to overtime. The old Browns of the early 2000s would have folded in overtime and lost, but this was the 2007 Super Browns and they were a different breed. Anderson led a drive that resulted in a 25–yard game winning field goal as the crowd came unglued and you could hear the cheers miles away. Anderson threw for 364 yards that game.

The albatross that season, like many others, remained Pittsburgh, as the Browns lost to them 31–28 the following week on the road. They would respond by winning four of their next five in the zaniest of ways. This included a last-second field goal win against Baltimore that was originally considered a miss before the refs reviewed and said Dawson nailed it for the win, a dramatic last-second win on the road against the Jets, and an 8–0 blizzard game victory over Buffalo at home. All of this ran their record to 9–5 as they traveled to Cincinnati for a week 15 showdown. Quite frankly, it should have been five straight wins had the Browns not gotten ripped off by the officials in a loss to the Cardinals that saw them take away a last-second touchdown catch from Winslow that would have won the game.

Still, they were 9–5 and just needed a win at Cincy to clinch a playoff berth. With the way everything lined up, this would have given them enough conference wins to clinch the berth in the playoffs. They simply needed to beat the lowly Bengals, who saw their season go down the drain after losing to the Browns in week 2. Cincy was currently 5–9 at the time and had nothing to play for but revenge.

Apparently, revenge was enough to motivate them as they jumped all over the Browns and led 19–0 at halftime. The Browns would rebound with two second half touchdown passes to Braylon Edwards to pull within 5 points at 19–14 with a little over 5 minutes to play. The Browns would get one more crack at a game-winning drive, but Derek Anderson and the Browns couldn't get it done. It was an awful game for Anderson that saw him throw four interceptions.

Because this was their sixth loss of the season, and their fifth AFC Conference loss, it made their final game meaningless the following week at home against San Francisco to close the season. It was a strange situation as they needed the Titans to lose to the Colts, and it wouldn't matter what they did against the 49ers. It was as odd as it gets. Sadly, for Cleveland, Colts head coach Tony Dungy pulled all of his starters early into the game, and the Titans won 16–10 on Sunday night football, effectively ending the Browns' season.

Despite missing the playoffs, 2007 will go down as one of the most fun and also successful seasons in Cleveland Browns history. Nearly a dozen players made the Pro Bowl, and young sensations like Kellen Winslow and Braylon Edwards finally met their full potential. Winslow finished with 1,106 yards on 82 catches with 5 touchdowns. Edwards caught 80 balls for 1,289 yards and an incredible 16 touchdowns. Had it not been for the magical season Tom Brady and Randy Moss had that year, Edwards would have had the best receiving stats in football along with Terrell Owens of Dallas. He was that good!

Jamal Lewis found the fountain of youth as they hoped he would, with 1,304 yards and 9 touchdowns on 298 attempts. Lewis also had two touchdown catches as he did it all when called upon. One unsung hero of the 2007 team was Joe Jurevicius who had 50 catches for 614 yards, but every single one of them was big. He was the chain mover and was counted on third down to get the yards needed each and every time. He had hands of glue, and was a calming leadership presence in the locker room.

The Browns had gone 10–6 and 7–1 at home. They swept the Ravens and it was their best record since returning to the league in 1999. Everything looked perfect and the talk of Super Bowl in 2008 was not far-fetched.

Sadly, for Cleveland, early into the 2008 season, everything went wrong and they never recovered. On the very first drive of their first preseason game against the Jets, Anderson led them on a touchdown drive that saw Edwards make an incredible touchdown catch. It was only preseason, but everything was looking great. That is when the weather gods took over and unleashed a severe thunderstorm only moments after

Hollie Strano had told everyone the skies would be clear. Players rushed off the field as fans ran for cover as well. Just like that, it was over in Cleveland.

Derek Anderson came back down to reality, only starting 9 games and throwing 9 touchdowns before being benched for Brady Quinn who ended up being a bust. Braylon Edwards only caught 55 balls and had a paltry 3 touchdowns. Kellen Winslow had a combination of injuries and attitude problems that held him to just 8 starts and 43 catches. He would end up trying to blame the Browns medical staff for his staph infection. The Browns had seven cases of staph infection in the last few years prior to this and Winslow was convinced Savage was hiding more.

Speaking of Savage, he was gone by season's end as well, when he responded to a fan's email by using a cuss word and telling them to go root for Buffalo. Crennel was gone shortly after the season ended as well. The Browns closed out the year with a 31–0 loss to the Steelers which began a longstanding tradition of firing the coach after a loss to Pittsburgh that would last for years.

The biggest knock on Crennel was the loose locker room that he ran. He had little to no discipline which was evident during training camp when highly touted free agent signing Donte Stallworth got his foot stepped on and injured by fellow wide receiver Braylon Edwards. Needing stiches, Stallworth missed a good chunk of time early into the season.

Stallworth had signed a seven-year, $35 million deal with the Cleveland Browns and was supposed to be the missing piece to lead them to the Super Bowl alongside Winslow and Edwards. However, he had just 17 catches for 170 yards and one touchdown for the Browns in 2008 and then missed the entire 2009 season after being suspended by the NFL following his conviction on manslaughter charges from drunk driving.

Still, even with Camp Romeo, Winslow and his attitude, the stone hands of Braylon Edwards, and the inconsistency of Derek Anderson, 2007 goes down as one of the most fun seasons in recent Cleveland Browns memory.

CHAPTER 4

# Baker Brings Back Relevancy

FOLLOWING THE 2008 LETDOWN, FOR THE BETTER PART OF THE NEXT decade, nothing went right for the Cleveland Browns as it was just one losing season after another, and the thoughts of 2007 and all that hope sailed further and further away. Rather than going season by season and giving everyone reading enough grief to cause an ulcer, I will skip to the *CliffsNotes* version. After Romeo Crennel and Phil Savage both left in 2008, here is everyone who showed up, failed, and was quickly sent packing.

*Head Coaches*

> Eric Mangini, 2009 and 2010, with a record of 10–22
>
> Pat Shurmur, 2011 and 2012, with a record of 9–23
>
> Rob Chudzinski, 2013, with a record of 4–12
>
> Mike Pettine, 2014 and 2015, with a record of 10–22
>
> Hugh Jackson, 2016, 2017, and part of 2018, with a record of 3–36–1

Thus, starting with Mangini in 2009 and going through Jackson's eight games in the 2018 season, that was almost a ten-year stretch with a record of 36–115–1, a winning percentage of less than 24 percent. That means they only won a game roughly every 4 to 5 times. It wasn't for lack of trying, though, as they brought in numerous young quarterbacks that came in with hype and much fanfare, only to fail miserably.

*Quarterbacks*

Colt McCoy in 2010

Brandon Weeden in 2012

Brian Hoyer in 2013

Johnny Manziel in 2014

Cody Kessler in 2016

DeShone Kizer in 2017

All of this went hand in hand with team presidents and GMs being hired just to be fired left and right. Men such as Mike Holmgren, Ray Farmer, Sashi Brown, Mike Lombardi, Tom Heckert, and George Kokinis in a revolving door.

Holmgren would come in at 11 a.m., get a massage in his office and then leave for the day. Farmer was texting the coach from the pressbox during games, telling him to put in players. Lombardi was an egomaniac, Heckert was drinking and driving, Kokinis was escorted from the premises by the police after eight games, and Brown created a team that went 1–31 in two seasons.

But at least the Browns tried to right the ship with strong veteran leadership at quarterback to mold all those younger names mentioned earlier. Each one, unfortunately, more broken down than the last. Former All Pros such as Jake Delhome, RG III, Jason Campbell, and Josh McCown just never worked out.

Heading into the 2018 season, the Browns were fresh off a stint on the HBO hit, *Hard Knocks*, and also fresh off of a horrific 0–16 season. Remarkably, team owner Jimmy Haslam elected to stick with 1–31 head coach Hugh Jackson, along with newly minted GM John Dorsey, to desperately right the ship.

Dorsey was credited with putting together the high-octane offense of the Kansas City Chiefs and the Browns had high hopes he could do it for them, too. He was gifted the first overall pick, via the 0–17 record, with all signs pointing to quarterback. The Browns also had the fourth pick in the draft, courtesy of a trade with Houston the year before, which resulted in the Texans acquiring Deshaun Watson.

Dorsey's first move of the 2018 offseason was to erase the quarterback room of the Browns as he dealt away Deshone Kizer to Green Bay and traded for Buffalo Bills quarterback Tyrod Taylor. Dorsey sent a 2018 third-round draft pick to the Bills. The odds were strong they would be taking a quarterback with the first overall pick, and they wanted a veteran to compete with him at camp, and also mold him. Taylor was that guy.

Taylor had been drafted in the sixth round by the Baltimore Ravens in the 2011 NFL Draft. He was nothing more than an afterthought out of Virginia Tech at that time. In four seasons with Baltimore, he took nineteen snaps as he learned behind Joe Flacco before finally getting a chance to start in Buffalo in 2015.

He would see the bulk of the snaps and the starts while with Buffalo in 2015, 2016, and 2017. He threw 15 touchdowns with the Bills next to only 16 interceptions. He was also a threat with his legs as he rushed for over 1,600 yards in 43 starts as a Buffalo Bill. While not making the playoffs, he was still a key cog in the Bill return to respectability as the franchise went 24–24 during that three-season stretch. A 500 winning percentage wasn't fantastic by any stretch, but it would mean eight more regular season wins than the Browns had in 2017 if he could do it in Cleveland.

Heading into the 2018 NFL Draft, the Browns were picking first overall for the second straight year. In 2017 they passed over possible franchise quarterbacks in Mitchell Trubisky who went second overall to Chicago, Patrick Mahomes who went tenth overall to Kansas City, and Deshaun Watson who went twelfth to Houston. Instead, they used the first overall pick on can't-miss defensive end Myles Garrett out of Texas A&M.

Garrett had 31 sacks and 141 tackles in his 3 years with the Aggies. It was a safe bet that Garrett would have a fine NFL career despite his injury-impacted first season with Cleveland. He only started 9 games his rookie season as a Brown and still had 7 sacks and countless quarterback hurries. He was also the most held pass rusher in the league and he was often double and triple teamed. It was far from his fault that the Browns went 0–16 in 2017.

John Dorsey had traded for All Pro wideout Jarvis Landry and only had to let go of a 2018 fourth-round draft pick. It was a giant steal for Cleveland to get Landry who caught exactly 400 passes in his 4 seasons in Miami with 22 touchdowns. He caught everything thrown to him, and never got hurt. Landry was the total package and ready to lead this young bunch.

Landry would just need someone to throw him the ball and even with Tyrod Taylor listed as the starter coming into camp, the eyes of John Dorsey remained on the draft. As the days drew near, it was clear the pick was down to Baker Mayfield out of Oklahoma, Sam Darnold out of USC, Josh Allen out of Wyoming, Josh Rosen out of UCLA, or Lamar Jackson our of Louisville. Each made a strong case for the number one pick, and it seemed as though Dorsey was in a no-lose situation.

Some fans wanted them to actually take stud running back Saquon Barkley out of Penn State with the number one pick, and then take the best remaining quarterback with the fourth pick. Barkley was the best running back prospect to come into the NFL since Adrian Peterson in 2007. Dorsey was sitting pretty no matter what decision he made as it was impossible for the Browns to go 0–16 two seasons in a row—they could only go up.

As a walk-on for the Lake Travis High School Cavaliers football team in Austin, Mayfield went 25–2 record in two seasons and won the 2011 4A State Championship. He finished his high school football career totaling 6,255 passing yards, 67 touchdowns, and 8 interceptions.

Mayfield loved the underdog role and flourished in it again in college at Texas Tech. While not originally the starter when he showed up in 2013, Mayfield became the first walk-on true freshman quarterback to start an FBS season opener at the quarterback position. Mayfield finished his freshman season with 2,315 yards on 218-of-340 completions with

12 touchdowns and 9 interceptions. He got hurt toward the end however, and lost his job to Davis Webb.

Mayfield earned Big 12 Conference Freshman Offensive Player of the Year for the 2013 season. However, in what seemed to be a common theme in his career, he took any possible slight as motivation and a reason for dissent. He was legitimately angry that he lost his starting job to injury, and Mayfield announced that he would be leaving the program due to a "miscommunication" with the coaching staff.

Texas Tech's loss was the Oklahoma Sooners' gain. Despite the fact that Mayfield was not eligible to play until the 2015 season, and he lost a season of eligibility due to Big 12 Conference transfer rules following an unsuccessful appeal of his transfer restrictions, he more than made up for it in 2016 and beyond. In these three seasons at center for the Sooners, he was nothing short of electric as he finished with 131 touchdowns and 14,607 yards.

In the 2017 Sugar Bowl, Mayfield helped lead the Sooners to a 35–19 victory over Auburn. He finished the game with 19 completions on 28 attempts for 296 passing yards and two touchdowns, earning him the MVP award. On December 9, 2017, Mayfield won the 2017 Heisman Trophy as he received 732 first-place votes and a total of 2,398 points. Mayfield is the first and only walk-on player to ever win the Heisman Trophy. If anyone ever fit the Cleveland Browns tough guy, everyman, underdog mantra, it was Baker Mayfield!

He was leaving college with a plethora of hardware. He was the 2017 Heisman Trophy winner and the 2017 Associated Press NCAA Player of the Year. He won the Manning award, the Maxwell award, the Walter Camp award, and the Davey O'Brien award, among over a dozen total awards during his time with Oklahoma.

He wasn't without his personality flaws, however. On September 9, 2017, after a win against the Ohio State Buckeyes in Columbus, Mayfield planted the Sooners' flag in the middle of the painted "O" at Ohio Stadium, causing a major public backlash. In November 2017, Mayfield was under fire again after an interaction during the game against Kansas. Mayfield was seen grabbing his crotch and mouthing "fuck you!" at the coach of the opposing team. He also told their fans to "go cheer on basketball team instead." He was also only 5 foot 10 inches, and quite frankly, fans worried he wouldn't be able to see over the line in the NFL.

John Dorsey didn't care or even want to hear about any of the downside, and snatched up Baker with the number one overall pick and then signed Mayfield to a four-year rookie contract with the Browns on July 24, 2018, with the deal worth $32.68 million in guaranteed salary. Dorsey got his man.

The Cleveland Browns were hideous to watch for nine straight seasons since the 2007 winning season. They hadn't made the playoffs since 2002 and they hadn't won a playoff game since 1994. They were fresh off of a 0–16 season and looking desperately everywhere for any reason at all, to have hope. Dorsey couldn't care less what body part Baker grabbed, or where he planted a flag; the Browns needed talent and Baker brought tons of it!

He had his quarterback and now it was time to make the fans even happier and send them into a frenzy. There is nothing Cleveland fans like better than rooting for one of their own, and they got that when Dorsey selected cornerback Denzel Ward out of Ohio State. Ward grew up in Macedonia and played his high school ball at Nordonia High School.

Ward wasn't just a local product; he was damn good, too! As a Buckeye he was First Team Big Ten in 2017, and a Consensus All American as teams stayed away from throwing the ball toward him. Need further proof of that? He only had to make twenty-three tackles his sophomore season with Ohio State, in thirteen games.

The loaded draft for the Browns didn't stop in the first round however, as they found a diamond in the rough with Nick Chubb in the second round. Chubb was absolutely electric as a Georgia Bulldog and it was insane that he was still sitting there in the second round. In four seasons as a Bulldog, he rushed for 4,769 yards and 44 touchdowns. He would have had more than that but he missed half the year his sophomore season with injury and had to split time with Sony Michel his final two seasons.

Michel would go on to be drafted by the Patriots, and bounce around to three teams in his first four years in the league. Meanwhile Chubb would go on to be one of the top backs in the NFL, rushing for 4,816 yards in 4 seasons, with 36 touchdowns.

Apparently, Dorsey didn't learn the lesson of the many GMs before him, as he also drafted much-maligned prospect Antonio Callaway out of Florida. The Gator, like Josh Gordon before him, was ultra-talented with wicked fast speed; the problem was his ability to stay clean. Between legal issues and drug issues, there was no guarantee he would ever see the field.

In his rookie year with the Browns, Callaway managed to play in all 16 games and was a force for them as well. He caught 43 balls for 586 yards and scored 5 touchdowns. He was the legit deep threat Baker Mayfield needed as he meshed well with sure-handed Jarvis Landry.

Sadly, for Callaway and the Browns, he wouldn't last long into a second season before they had to cut all ties with him. On August 9, 2019, Callaway was suspended for the first four games of the 2019 season for violating the NFL's substance abuse policy. Once he was back, his attitude and behavior got worse as he overslept for meetings. He was also facing a ten-game suspension at the time of his release because of drug issues, multiple substances found in his car that were allegedly being transported from Florida by a different driver.

Never had fans cheered a tie like they did week 1 of the 2018 season when the Cleveland Browns came back to tie the Pittsburgh Steelers to open the season. Down 21–7 in the fourth quarter, with under eight minutes to play, it looked as though the Browns would lose yet another opener to start the season. Although this time, Tyrod Taylor refused to give up as he led back-to-back fourth quarter drives to send it into overtime.

First it was another former Ohio State Buckeye, Carlos Hyde, pounding it in from 1 yard out to cut the lead to 21–14. Then, about 4 minutes later, Taylor found Josh Gordon from 17 yards out, to tie the game at 21 with 1:56 to play.

Both teams had a chance to win it in overtime but both met with missed field goal attempts. Steeler kicker Chris Boswell had his blocked from forty-two yards out, setting up great field position for the Browns to try and win it. A few plays later, it was Zane Gonzalez missing badly from forty-three yards out for Cleveland. This was a sign of things to come for Gonzalez and the Browns.

Despite not winning, they finally avoided losing to their rivals, and even though Baker Mayfield didn't get the start, something still felt different, like a new era was born in Cleveland as rookie Denzel Ward picked off Big Ben twice. Those feelings of positivity sailed away the next week when they blew a 12–3 fourth quarter lead on the road in New Orleans, falling to the Saints 21–18 in dramatic fashion.

The Saints had come back to take the 18–12 lead on the Browns following a Drew Brees to Michael Thomas touchdown pass with 2:40 to go in the game. Yet again, it felt like the "same old Browns" mantra with the blown fourth quarter lead. But again, 2018 represented the new era of football in Cleveland and they kept fighting. They scored on a shocking long ball to Antonio Callaway as Taylor found him streaking wide open down the middle of the field from forty-seven yards out to tie the game with a circus-like catch. Zane Gonzales missed the extra point however, and kept the game tied at 18.

Sure enough, the Saints drove for a game-wining field goal by Will Lutz from 44 yards out with 21 seconds to go. But again, this Browns team was different and didn't stop fighting. After a touchback, Taylor hit Jarvis Landry on a cross over the middle for 25 quick yards. Then, it was Callaway catching one for 16 yards, and just like that, the Browns had a chance to tie it with a 52-yard field goal. Zane Gonzales missed again, and the Browns took the loss.

In regard to Gonzales, many fans didn't even want him on the plane ride home. It was a horrific game for Gonzales in the dome, as he went 0 for 2 on extra points, and 2 of 4 on field goals. If he would have made any combination of those 4 missed kicks, the Browns would have won, or at the very least, forced another overtime game. Gonzalez was cut by the next day, and the petition to bring Phil Dawson, yet unsuccessful, was started.

Heading into NFL Thursday Night Football against the New York Jets, it almost seemed like a Hollywood script was about to play out. It had all the makings of a classic as the Jets were terrible, and were starting Sam Darnold as their quarterback. Darnold was the man many thought the Browns would select until they changed course at the last second and selected Mayfield. Adding fuel to the fire, it was Darnold and former Cleveland Brown Isaiah Crowell helping New York build a 14–0 lead in the first half.

Crowell played well for the Browns during his four previous seasons in Cleveland before departing in the 2017–2018 offseason for New York. He never ran for 1,000 yards, but never had the chance as during that stretch of time, the Browns consistently had to throw the ball all second half long because of large deficits. Crowell was a producer on the field for the Browns, but ran into a bit of trouble off the field with some comments. In July 2016, following the deaths of Alton Sterling and Philando Castile, Crowell posted on his Instagram a controversial violent image of a faceless person dressed in black who was slitting the throat of a captive law enforcement officer with a knife; he later had the photo deleted and apologized for his actions.

Down 14–0, the crowd was chanting for Baker, Baker, Baker to get in the game. Tyrod Taylor was 4 of 14 at this point, and had been sacked 3 times. In two and half games as quarterback, Taylor had gone 42 of 85 passing with 2 touchdowns and 2 interceptions. Not exactly a world beater!

This is why, when Baker Mayfield checked into the game with 1:42 to play in the first half and the Browns trailing, First Energy Stadium came unglued. Why he wasn't starting from week 1 was anyone's guess, but now Hugh Jackson had no choice but to play him as Taylor was injured.

Just as an epic Hollywood blockbuster would play out, Mayfield saved the day and instantly leapt into of the hearts of Browns fans around the globe. Mayfield was flawless, finishing the game 17 of 23 for 201 yards and only getting sacked once. He didn't turn the ball over, and was razor sharp in his decision making. His fundamentals were sound and he looked brilliant as he led the Browns back to win the game 21–17 with a fourth-quarter closing minute touchdown drive. The Cleveland Browns had found their franchise quarterback.

As Baker Mayfield stole the hearts of Clevelanders everywhere, it was now time for another rookie to leap onto the page starting the next week in Oakland. Heading into the game against the Raiders, Nick Chubb had only run the ball 7 times for 41 yards, for a ridiculous 5.8-yard average. It was no fluke as he went for 105 yards on only 3 carries with 2 touchdowns. His touchdown runs of 41 and 63 yards pretty much meant the Browns had found their new starting tailback, and the days of Carlos Hyde were now numbered.

It was a wild affair that appeared as though the Browns sealed it in regulation up 42–34 with a minute to play. They converted a fourth and one that should have sealed the game. For reasons never quite explained, the clear-cut first down was reviewed in New York by the league officials, and then promptly overturned. The Raiders would go on to tie the game and then win it in overtime, erasing the 295-yard, 2-touchdown performance from Baker.

If Zane Gonzales could make a field goal, they would have beaten Pittsburgh and New Orleans. If the NFL hadn't overturned the first down in Oakland, they would have been 4–0 after four weeks. As it stood however, they were 1–2–1 as they hosted Baltimore week 5 back home. It was another overtime affair; this time Baker led the game-winning drive as Greg Joseph barely made a 37-yard field goal with two seconds left in overtime to give them their second win.

Despite the win, Chubb only had three carries and the faith in "offensive genius" Hugh Jackson was starting to fade. For good reason too, as the Browns went on to lose their next three games, falling to 2–5–1 at the eight-game mark, and leading to the dismissal of Hugh Jackson after a 33–18 road loss to Pittsburgh. Jimmy Haslam continued the longstanding tradition of firing the coach after a loss to the Steelers. Defensive coordinator Gregg Williams took over as head coach and Freddie Kitchens stepped into the offensive coordinator role with the termination of Todd Haley.

The moves were genius, and following a loss to powerhouse Kansas City, they went on to win five of their next six games, improving their record to 7–7–1 heading into the season closer at Baltimore. They were red hot as Baker Mayfield and Nick Chubb both took off with Hugh Jackson no longer around to hold them both back.

Despite the loss at Baltimore to close the season at 7–8–1, Browns fans were hyped out of their minds at the incredible seven-win improvement in just one year, and the 7–7 record they put up in games where Baker took the majority of the snaps. Speaking of Baker, he finished with a rookie record 3,725 yards and 27 touchdowns. The franchise quarterback was here to stay!

Mayfield wasn't the only new addition that lit it up. Nick Chubb rushed for 996 yards on just 192 carries for an incredible 5.2 yards per carry average. He also caught 20 balls for 149 yards and two scores. Jarvis Landry was not only a vocal leader in the locker room, but also a production leader, as he finished with 81 catches for 976 yards and 4 touchdowns.

Mayfield got the best out of Hollywood Higgins, who had done nothing in his first two years with the Browns, only catching 33 balls, to bust out with Baker in 2018 for 39 catches and 572 yards. The nucleus of the Browns moving forward was formed and looking great.

Gregg Williams led the Browns to a 5–3 record during his time as head coach, but he was seen as a knucklehead and borderline psychotic behind the scenes, so they opted to move on from him after the season in favor of popular assistant coach Freddie Kitchens. A lot of insiders actually credited Kitchens' play calling and offensive schemes for the Browns improvement in 2018.

The Browns were the most hyped team in the NFL heading into the 2019 season. They had a record breaker with Baker Mayfield, a stud running back with Nick Chubb and a defensive monster with Myles Garrett. The hype was warranted and then took to the next level when they acquired troubled but extremely talented wideout Odell Beckham Jr. from the New York Giants. The Browns sent 2017 first-round pick and bust Jabril Peppers alongside Kevin Zeitler, the Browns' first-round pick, and their second third-round pick in the 2019 NFL Draft, in exchange for Odell Beckham Jr. and Olivier Vernon.

It all seemed perfect as OBJ was the most physically talented wideout in the NFL and needed to get away from the aging Eli Manning in New York. He was a genetic freak, ultra-popular and just happened to be the best friend of Jarvis Landry. What could possibly go wrong?

Adding the cherry to the sundae, John Dorsey rolled the dice and acquired Toledo Rocket and former Kansas City Chief, Kareem Hunt, amid major controversy. Hunt was released by the Chiefs on November 30, 2018, after a videotape of him physically assaulting a woman and kicking her on the ground the previous February surfaced. Hunt was never charged with any crime, as the incident was investigated as a misdemeanor assault and the victim failed to properly take her case to court. The NFL was still upset and Hunt would be facing an eight-game suspension once he returned to the league in 2019.

Hunt was signed by the Cleveland Browns on February 11, 2019. Due to the pending investigation from the NFL into the assault allegations against him, Hunt was placed on the Commissioner's Exempt list after signing his contract. On March 15, 2019, the NFL announced that Hunt had been suspended without pay for the first eight games of the 2019 season for violating the league's personal conduct policy. He was eligible to participate in all off-season workouts and all preseason games, which would give the Browns a small sample size of what he could do.

Hunt was ultra-talented as he excelled locally at Willoughby South High School where he graduated in 2013 and then attended Toledo. In his time as a Rocket, he rushed for 4,945 yards and 44 touchdowns as he was one of the greatest MAC Conference running backs of all time.

His success continued with Kansas City. In his first 27 games as a Chief before getting suspended and cut from the team, he rushed for 2,151 yards and 15 touchdowns. He also caught 79 balls for nearly 1,000 yards and 10 touchdowns as he was the top pass catching back in the league. In his rookie year, he had secured the rushing title with 1,327 yards. He was now a Cleveland Brown.

Even with all the hype, nothing went right in 2019, starting with a 43–13 blowout loss to Tennessee at home to open the season with another loss. Eight games in, they had fallen to 2–6 and all hope was pretty much gone. They managed a midseason winning streak but even that was halted when Myles Garrett lost his ever-loving mind and assaulted Pittsburgh Steeler quarterback Mason Rudolph with his helmet on Thursday Night Football. Garrett literally took Rudolph's helmet off and bashed him with it, landing an instant season-long suspension with the league.

The Browns finished with a 6–10 record. Nick Chubb ran for 1,494 yards but that was one of the few things to actually work out. Mayfield never formed chemistry with OBJ, as Beckham only had 74 catches for 1035 and just 4 touchdowns. Mayfield tossed 22 touchdowns, but that was next to 21 interceptions and some seriously shaky play throughout the season. Freddie Kitchens and John Dorsey were both let go following the season, opening the door for a new coach to take over an extremely talented team that simply needed direction.

# CHAPTER 5

# Playoffs

WHILE FANS CLAMORED FOR JOSH McDANIEL, LINCOLN RILEY, OR Michael McCarthy to take over the team as head coach and GM, the Browns went analytical instead, hiring Harvard graduate Andrew Berry as general manager. They also hired Minnesota offensive coordinator Kevin Stefanski. Fans were lukewarm about both hires, but both would prove to be tremendous moves.

Both men were taking over a team already built to win with a loaded roster. Good for them that it would need to be "ready made," because the 2020 offseason was like none other with no minicamps, OTAs, or even preseason games. The COVID-19 pandemic put a stop to all of that, and Zoom meetings became the new way to communicate and study playbooks.

One thing they knew for certain was that if Baker Mayfield was going to perform at a high caliber, he was going to need time in the pocket to stay upright. Mayfield looked jittery and rushed far too many times in 2019, and they needed him under control and focused if this team was going to have any chance at competing in the stacked AFC North.

With that being the case, it was of surprise that they used their first-round pick in the 2020 NFL Draft to select offensive tackle Jedrick Wills out of Alabama with the tenth overall pick. He was only the second tackle to come off the board behind Andrew Thomas from Georgia who went to the New York Giants. This was a huge steal for the Browns as he was seen as the best tackle in the draft by many pundits, and on the overall top five boards of most mock drafts.

Wills was named a first team preseason All-American by Athlon Sports and to the second team by the Associated Press, the Sporting News, *Sports Illustrated*, and *USA Today* entering his junior season. Wills was named a first team midseason All-American by the Associated Press. He was named first team All-SEC and was a consensus second team All-America selection at the end of the season after starting all of the Crimson Tide's games and missing only seven total blocking assignments in 771 total snaps played. He was a perfect fit for the Browns run first and grind it out offense. They had craved a solid Left Tackle since Browns legend Joe Thomas retired after the 0–16, 2017 season.

He was on the 2017 National Champion Alabama Crimson Tide team. He was a second team All-American in 2019 and First Team All Sec in 2019 as well. Wills was now a Cleveland Brown who brought a winning tradition and culture with him from college. They would need that type of thing in a huddle that featured highly explosive personalities such as Baker Mayfield and OBJ.

Not only would the drafting of Wills be key for the Browns, but so would the signing of free agent right tackle Jack Conklin. Conklin signed a three-year, $42 million contract with the Cleveland Browns after spending his first four years in the league with the Tennessee Titans. He was named to the All-Rookie Team and an All Pro in 2016. The Browns were hoping he could reclaim some of that early 2016 magic that he had, before tearing his ACL in 2018 with the Titans.

Upgraded line protection was something Mayfield badly needed; he had to be comfortable in that pocket. In 2019, the line was plagued with injuries and it seemed like a revolving door at left tackle and numerous other spots on the line. Starting the season with a strong line, and some new threats to go with it, was the plan of new GM Andrew Barry to make sure Mayfield had zero excuses this time around.

One of the new threats they brought in for Baker to throw the ball to was four-year pro Austin Hooper from the Atlanta Falcons. Hooper had been with the Falcons since being drafted out of Stanford in 2016. He was one of the top tight ends in free agency. Hooper was coming off of a big 2019 season with 75 receptions for 787 receiving yards and 6 receiving touchdowns. The Browns signed him to a 4-year deal worth $44 million, with a $10 million signing bonus.

This was just part of the plan to increase the threats Baker had out there at all times. The Browns' brass was clearly not happy with their current starting tight end David Njoku whose first three seasons in the league had been plagued by injuries and dropped balls. They further expressed their frustration with Njoku by selecting fellow tight end Harrison Bryant in the fourth round of the 2020 NFL Draft out of Florida Atlantic.

While Bryant was known as a possession-style sure hands tight end, their receiving threat selected in the 2020 NFL Draft was known for big plays. In the sixth round with their final pick they selected Michigan do-it-all man, Donovan Peoples Jones. He was electric in college while playing for the Michigan Wolverines and the Browns were hoping to catch some of that Josh Cribbs magic with him, once again becoming deadly in the punt and kick returns games.

Jones, in just his third game at Michigan, returned two punts for 104 yards, including a 79-yard return for a touchdown in the third quarter against Air Force. His 79-yard return for a touchdown was the longest by any Michigan punt returner since Steve Breaston went 83 yards against Indiana in 2006. It was the part of a massive freshman season at Michigan in which he finished with the second-most return attempts and eighth-most return yards in a single season by a Wolverine, and also caught 22 passes for 277 yards. He was also named a Freshman All-American by Football Writers Association of America and 247 Sports, and was named Michigan's Rookie of the Year.

He was just getting started, as in his sophomore season he showed everyone he was much more than just a returner and could play meaningful downs at wide receiver as well. During the 2018 season, Peoples-Jones led the team with 39 receptions, for 541 yards and 7 touchdowns. He also remained a force on special teams with a punt return average of (10.1) among players with 10 returns or more, and his 64 career return attempts ranks fourth in Michigan program history.

Nothing would change his junior year in 2019 as he just kept show-ing up and showing out. He was named to the All-Big Ten special teams third-team by the media, and the All-Big Ten offensive team honorable mention by the media. All of this success convinced him to forego his final season of eligibility to enter the 2020 NFL draft.

The Browns lost veteran and fan-favorite linebackers Joe Schobert and Christian Kirksey in free agency. While fans were sad to see them go, they welcomed in a slew of veteran defensive players via free agency as well.

The Browns added Andrew Billings from the Bengals at defensive tackle. They brought in Adrian Clayborn from the Falcons to play defen-sive end and they also added secondary help by signing defensive backs Karl Joseph from the Raiders and Kevin Johnson from the Buffalo Bills. These signings went nicely with 2020 NFL Draft picks Grant Delpit, a safety out of LSU, along with linebacker out of LSU Jacob Phillips and tackle out of Missouri Jordan Elliot.

The Browns hoped to achieve better results with these two LSU draft picks than they did with 2019 NFL Draft selection Greedy Williams. They took Williams with their first pick in the second round in 2019 as they had traded their first-round pick to the Giants for OBJ. Williams came in with a ton of hype and had a horrendous 2019 season, marred with injuries and lack of production. The numbers after 12 games for Williams were horrendous, with only 37 tackles and 0 interceptions, also only 2 pass breakups. He would go on to miss the entire 2020 season with injuries as well.

I'd be remiss if I didn't bring up one memorable player named "The Scottish Tack Hammer." In a classic case of "rugby player turned foot-ball star," originally from Inverness, Gillan first played for Highland Rugby Club before attending and playing rugby for Merchiston Castle School in Edinburgh. In 2013, he moved to Leonardtown, Maryland, where his father was stationed as a member of the Royal Air Force, and Gillan began playing American football in high school.

He parlayed his new love of American football into a scholarship he received though a Facebook workout video sent to Arkansas–Pine Bluff where Gillan had a total of 9,024 yards on 214 punts and average of 42.2 yards per punt. So strong was the leg of the "Hammer" that he actually popped three balls during an NFL pre-draft workout. Complete with long mullet styled out of his helmet and an extremely lanky frame at well over six feet, there was no way this guy wasn't getting noticed by American football clubs.

The Browns signed him as an undrafted rookie in 2020 and were wise to do so. Gillan ended his rookie season with 63 punts for 2,913 yards (2,622 net yards) with 28 punts downed inside the 20-yard line which earned him a spot on the Pro Football Writers Association All-Rookie team. Not only that, but even before the season could begin, with the knowledge of his rugby history known, fans were screaming for at least one fake punt from the Hammer.

The Browns were set to begin another season with plenty of hype and hope, but this time in front of no fans as they started the season in Baltimore. Maryland was one of the states in which zero fans would be allowed at any sports gathering due to the pandemic.

While the rest of the country worried about COVID-19 and mask mandates, the Browns were trying to win football games with a first-year head coach, and next to zero time together in the offseason to prepare. Everyone hates preseason games, but after the opening week loss to Baltimore 38–6, the Browns sure looked like they could have used at least a few tune-up quarters.

It was dreadful, as Baker Mayfield was picked off once, sacked twice and held to 189 yards on 21 of 29 passing. It wasn't all Mayfield's fault however as once again, OBJ couldn't get open and was held to 3 catches for 22 yards. Kareem Hunt and Nick Chubb combined for 132 yards on 23 carries but it wasn't nearly enough to even keep pace with Lamar Jackson and the Ravens.

Jackson gave the Browns fits all day long as they couldn't do anything to stop him. Jackson threw for 275 yards, 3 touchdowns and ran for 45 more yards. The Browns defensive coordinator Joe Woods had zero answers. Adding insult to injury, rookie tailback J. K. Dobbins ran for two touchdowns on the Browns defense. Browns fans weren't shocked they lost, but no one saw it coming that badly.

While placekicker Austin Seibert wasn't the cusp of the problem, he sure wasn't helping anything either. If you recall, he missed his first extra point attempt the previous year in the opener against Tennessee, and everything then went immediately south. This season would be no different, as the Browns' only touchdown on the day, a pass from Mayfield to Njoku, would only equate to six points after Seibert missed the extra point and the Browns wouldn't score again.

He had a decent rookie year in 2019 when he went 25 of 29 on fields and 30 of 35 on extra points. The Browns weren't messing around this season and waiting for him to get it as Seibert was waived by the Browns on September 14, 2020, after missing a field goal and extra point in a 38–6 loss to the Baltimore Ravens. The extra misses were just killers, and Andrew Barry and Kevin Stefanski weren't going to put up with it. His 499 points were the most of any kicker in the FBS history while in college at Oklahoma. But that was then, this was now, and he was gone.

If the Browns were going to bring in a kicker, they were not going to have a ton of time to pick one as their next game was that Thursday night at home against rookie Joe Burrow and the Cincinnati Bengals. Ironically enough, Seibert signed with the Bengals the day after the Browns cut him. Meanwhile the Browns signed Cody Parkey, whose infamous "double doink" cost the Chicago Bears a playoff game following the 2018 regular season.

As the episode of "Kicker Carousel" took place, the Browns defense needed to adjust and adjust quickly, as the last thing they wanted to do was hand the 2020 NFL Draft overall first pick, Joe Burrow, his first professional win. Burrow did his best to continue on the success he had at LSU where he won a Heisman by throwing for 316 yards and three touchdowns in his first nationally televised game. The only reason he didn't light up the Browns for more was he had a faulty offensive line that allowed him to be sacked three times, one of which he fumbled.

The Browns, for their credit, would escape with the 35–30 win as they staved off a last-second Joe Burrow comeback attempt. The Orange and Brown offense did their thing that night for the home opener as Baker Mayfield threw for 219 yards and 2 touchdowns with another interception. OBJ came out for a 4 catch, 74 performance, with a 43-yard touchdown.

The biggest reason for the victory that more than made up for a mediocre Mayfield performance and shaky defense was the dynamic duo of Kareem Hunt and Nick Chubb in the backfield. They both went off to combine for 210 yards on 23 carries with 3 touchdowns. Kareem Hunt also had a touchdown through the air as well. This was an early indicator that when Chubb and Hunt were used in a steady onslaught of offense, few teams could stop them, if any at all.

The steady run game along with smart play calling by Stefanski sparked wins over the Washington Football Team at home and then against the Cowboys on the road and the Colts back at home to start the season 4–1 on the heels of a four-game winning streak. Yes, you're reading that correctly: the Browns started 4–1 and fans were printing playoff tickets!

The win over Washington at home featured a fourth-quarter comeback in which they outscored the former Skins 17–0 in the final quarter to win 34–20. It was another week where Baker was bailed out by incredible rushing from Hunt and Chubb; he combined for nearly 200 yards on the ground and 3 total touchdowns between the two.

The spotlight win, and the performance Browns fans had been dreaming of since the second they traded for OBJ in 2019, took place in Dallas. The Browns defeated the Cowboys, 49–38, in one of the craziest games in franchise history. OBJ would go for 73 yards rushing with the game capping touchdown, along with 5 catches for 81 yards and 2 more touchdowns. This was the OBJ that the Browns has been waiting twenty-plus games to show up. Over 150 combined yards and three total touchdowns. It was better late than never for their superstar.

As mentioned, the game itself was pure insanity. After a thirty-seven-yard touchdown pass to OBJ put them ahead 7–0 on the game's first drive, it was time for Dallas go off. The Cowboys would score the next fourteen points with touchdown passes from Dak Prescott to Amari Cooper and CeeDee Lamb. During the same stretch that saw the Browns fall behind to close the first quarter, it also saw Nick Chubb go down to injury.

The old Browns would have crumbled on the road against America's team without their best player. This was not the same old Browns and they were about to show everyone why. They put up twenty-four points in a dream second quarter that saw Mayfield touchdown passes to OBJ and Austin Hooper while Kareem Hunt pounded in a touchdown run. Cody Parked nailed a thirty-seven-yard field goal as time ran out and the Browns took a 31–14 lead into the half.

The Browns aimed to erase all doubt and prove they were for real when they poured on 10 more third quarter points to take a 41–14 lead into the fourth quarter. Up by 27 points, it should have been a safe lead to begin the fourth, but the Browns proceeded to let up 24 straight points, on 3 straight Cowboy touchdowns and 3 straight 2-point conversions. It was suddenly 41–38 with nearly 4 minutes still left to play.

OBJ had already leapt into the hearts of Browns fans earlier in the day with his incredible performance catching the ball and he was about to do it again, this time with his feet as he rattled off a fifty-yard touchdown run on an end around that originally looked like it was going to be a major loss of yardage. OBJ used speed and just plain raw talent to break away from would-be tacklers in the backfield and then all the way to the endzone. A few minutes later a Denzel Ward intercept would seal it.

The 32–23 victory at home over the Colts improved them to 3–0 in Cleveland and came on the strength of veteran quarterback Phillip Rivers along with a forty-seven-yard pick six from defensive back Ronnie Harrison. They were able to beat a tough defense in the Colts, without their star tailback Nick Chubb who had to miss the game with injury.

A 38–7 blowout loss at Heinz Field to the Steelers had fans hanging their heads low; the first half the following week against the Bengals had them on the verge of tears. A Baker Mayfield misplaced ball about two feet behind OBJ caused Beckham to get hurt trying to make a tackle off the interception. Beckham tore his ACL, and was done for the year just like that. The Browns were also trailing 10–3 on the road.

While some fans choose to remember the poorly thrown ball by Baker Mayfield, others choose to focus on the point that he went for five touchdowns, with 297 yards in an epic performance. Following the OBJ injury, Baker made every single big throw and looked like the second coming of Joe Montana. With OBJ out, he tossed the 5 touchdowns, 2 of them while behind in the fourth quarter, and at one point 20 straight completions.

The winning touchdown toss went to Donovan Peoples Jones from 37 yards out with 11 seconds to go as Baker and this new version of the Kardiac Kids did it again! Without OBJ, DPJ shined with 3 catches for 56 yards and a touchdown. Tight end Harrison Bryant also had 56 yards receiving and 2 touchdowns to go along with fellow tight end David Njoku's 1 touchdown performance. Kareem Hunt caught a touchdown pass in the big day from Baker. Browns fans hated to admit it, but it would become crystal clear as time went on: Mayfield was simply much better without OBJ in the lineup.

It was a crazy way to start the season, filled with ups and down including injuries to star players Nick Chubb and OBJ, but all that aside, the Browns were 5–2 and hadn't had a start that hot since returning to the league in 1999. This is also when the "wind-soaked homestand" came into play. The Browns played three straight games at home in extremely windy conditions that saw them go 2–1 in that stretch.

They lost to the Las Vegas Raiders 16–6 before defeating Houston 10–7 and Philly 22–17. It was perhaps the most boring three-game stretch in First Energy Stadium history. The Raiders game was dominated on the ground by Vegas, the Browns only had the ball for 47 plays the entire game. The Browns had the ball only 6 times all game. Just 6 possessions as they simply couldn't get off the field on third down.

The victory over Houston was so incredibly lackluster that it was only 3–0 Cleveland after three quarters. Despite the lack of scoring, it couldn't be ignored that a healthy Nick Chubb was back as he and Kareem Hunt both ran for 100 plus yards each. Hunt ran for 104 yards on 19 carries while 126 yards on 19 carries with the game-sealing 59-yard scamper to run out the clock.

If the weather made for a boring game the week prior with Houston, the next week with Philly in town wasn't exactly a thriller, either. Once again, the first half saw next to no scoring as 7–0 at half, following another scoreless first quarter and almost scoreless first half. The Browns ground out the victory with another 114 yards on the ground from Nick Chubb.

It wasn't pretty, but who cared; the Browns were 7–3 and that's all that mattered. The winning streak continued the following week at Jacksonville 27–25 in a game that saw six lead changes. Once again, they had to hang on in the closing seconds as the comparison to the Kardiac Kids continued.

Heading into week 12, the Browns were 8–3 but the consistent knock was that they weren't beating anyone with a winning record. Everyone they beat had a losing record with the only exception being the victory over Indianapolis. They would get a serious chance to silence the critics as they arrived in Tennessee for a showdown with the 8–3 Titans.

Not only was this a chance to defeat a quality opponent on the road, but it was also a chance to get revenge on the team that instantly crushed their dreams a year ago with a demoralizing opening week blowout loss. In almost an exact repeat of the Dallas game—the Browns built a huge lead and then had to hold on for dear life to win. This time it was Cleveland up 38–7 at half in a massive whitewash. Then, the Titans came back like a hurricane in the second half to cut it to 41–35 before the Browns escaped and salvaged the win.

Despite the scary ending, once again, a win was a win and the Browns were 9–3, but because the AFC North was so loaded, they were still in third place in their division. The following week the Browns would lose on Monday Night Football 47–42 to their rivals, the Baltimore Ravens. They appeared to have won on a Baker Mayfield last-minute fourth quarter touchdown drive with 64 seconds on the clock, which is all it took for Justin Tucker to break their hearts with a 55-yard field goal. Mayfield was electric that night with 343 yards and 2 touchdowns, but once again, the Browns defense couldn't stop Lamar Jackson.

The Browns would close out the year with a convincing 20–6 Sunday Night Football win on the road against the Giants. A shocking loss to the Jets 23–16 and then a dream come true victory at home over Pittsburgh sealed the playoff berth. Each game had a different storyline, as the win over the Giants came against former coach Freddie Kitchens and quarterback Colt McCoy. The loss to the Jets was due to the entire wide receiving core being wiped out by COVID protocol.

When the final snap was taken by Baker Mayfield to down the ball and seal the 24–22 victory over Pittsburgh, the 12,000 fans in attendance sounded like 120,000 as First Energy Stadium and all of Cleveland came unglued. The Browns were 11–5 and headed back to the playoffs for the first time since 2002.

This game, like many of the prior ones in 2020, was a down-to-the-wire win for Cleveland. This time, the Browns built a 24–9 fourth-quarter lead before watching the Steelers score thirteen straight points to cut it to 24–22 with 1:23 to go. The Browns recovered the onside kick, eventually converted a first down, and it was time to celebrate!

Ironically, the 11–5 record brought them a rematch with Pittsburgh on the road the following week at Heinz Field. They hadn't won at Heinz Field since a Sunday night in October of 2003. Since then, it was seventeen straight years of losing in Pittsburgh at the Ketchup Bottle. Perhaps luck would be on their side this time around.

They would need good luck as the week started off with bad news when they found out head coach Kevin Stefanski would have to enter COVID-19 protocol and miss the game. Yet again, Cleveland teams in years past would crumble with this sort of adversity, but not this team, not this year!

In what seemed to be the theme of their season, the Browns built a massive first half lead, and then clung to life in the final moments for the victory. This time around, the Browns jumped all over the Steelers as the very first snap of the game saw the ball hiked ten feet over Big Ben's head and chased down by Karl Joseph for a Browns touchdown. It wouldn't get any better for Ben as a series of turnovers and miscues led to a 35–7 first half lead.

A wild second half comeback for the Steelers would come up short as the Browns prevailed 48–37. It wasn't lack of trying for Big Ben however as he threw for 501 yards in a record-setting performance. The problem was, 501 yards and 4 touchdowns are great, but 4 interceptions and a fumble can ruin any performance and it did on this night as he couldn't stop throwing the ball to Browns defenders.

It may not have been 500 yards, but there was nothing wrong with the night Mayfield had. Baker launched 3 touchdown passes along with 263 yards on 21 of 34 passing. You can say the defense set him up to succeed with incredible field position time after time, or you could say he stepped up in the moment. One thing couldn't be debated, however, and that is the Browns won the game and the winning days of Cleveland football were finally back to stay!

# PART II

# THE STARS AND THE RIVALRIES

# CHAPTER 6

# The Prime Time Browns!

As a little kid growing up in the 1980s and 1990s, I'll never forget how cool it was watching those helmets collide right at 9 p.m. every Monday night for seventeen straight weeks in the fall and winter to symbolize Monday Night Football was on. It was the only night of the week I was allowed to stay up far past my normal bedtime. To this day, prime time football remains one of my favorite treasures as a sports fan. In recent years, Sunday Night Football has replaced Monday Night Football as the biggest and best game of the week, but both nights remain must-watch!

The great thing about being a Browns fan is that, despite how bad the team has been since its return to the NFL in 1999, because of the incredible fan base and history, we still have had our share of great prime time games. In fact, what few people realize is that former owner Art Modell was instrumental in bringing Monday Night Football to national television in the first place. It was he who brought it to fruition and it was no shock that the Cleveland Browns hosted the New York Jets in the first-ever Monday Night Football game held on September 21, 1970.

The Browns won that night, 31–21, over the visiting New York Jets. It was a very late start to the season, but the Monday Night showcase made the wait worth it. The Browns jumped out to a 14–0 lead in the first quarter thanks in part to an eight-yard touchdown pass from Gary Collins to Bill Nelson. Later in the quarter it was tailback Bo Scott taking it in from two yards out to extend the lead to 14–0.

The Jets held the Browns scoreless in the second quarter as they cut into the lead 14–7 with an Emerson Boozer five-yard touchdown run. If the Browns wanted to give the national television audience something special to remember, they did just that as they opened the second half by taking the Jets kickoff to the house as Homer Jones caught the kick and went ninety-seven yards to score.

Down 21–7, Broadway Joe Namath attempted to lead a comeback. He and the Jets cut the lead to 24–21 with possession of the ball and attempting a game-winning drive in the closing moments. It was then the Browns who gave the Prime Time Nation and hometown fans something to remember them by as Billy Andrews picked off the Namath pass and took it back for a 25-yard touchdown to seal the game.

The Browns won 31–21 with fourteen of those points coming on defense and special teams. Their defense picked off Joe Namath three times throughout the night. He did throw for 298 yards in the Jets loss. Namath was helped out by Matt Snell who ran for 108 yards on 16 carries but it wasn't nearly enough.

It wasn't the only Browns' appearance on Monday Night that season as the Oilers would come to town to visit the 5–6 Browns in week 12. The Browns overcame a horrendous performance by quarterback Bill Nelsen who threw 2 interceptions and only for 161 yards on 15 of 27 passing. The Browns were powered that night by Leroy Kelley who toted the ball for 108 yards and a touchdown in the 21–10 win.

One year into the phenom known as "Monday Night Football," the Browns were a quick 2–0 in prime time. They had a tremendous 1971 season that saw them go 9–5 but lose their only prime time game to the Oakland Raiders. The silver and black would go on to haunt the Browns several more times in the coming decades.

The Browns took their prime time luck to the road in 1973 with a thrilling 21–17 win at the San Diego Chargers. This wasn't the legendary Super Chargers team that featured Dan Fouts and Kellen Winslow Sr. and that showed, as only five Chargers touched the ball the entire game. Quarterback John Hadl only completed twelve passes all game, and the Browns defense only allowed five of the passes to go to wide receivers.

Browns quarterback Mike Phipps wasn't exactly a world beater that evening either, as he only went 12 of 21 for the game with a touchdown toss to Frank Pitts from 38 yards with only moments to play. The Browns overcame two deficits in that game to come from behind and win on the road. They would finish the season 10–4 but lose to Miami in the playoffs.

Speaking of Miami, the Browns lost to them in their only MNF appearance in 1973, a 17–9 road loss. That defeat came as part of a 7–5–2 season that would fall short of the playoffs. This sparked a series of losses that wouldn't see the Browns return to Monday Night Football until the 1977 season.

This clash came week 2 of the season as the Browns hosted the New England Patriots. They spotted the Pats a 17–7 halftime lead. A Brian Sipe touchdown pass to Gary Parris combined with a field goal from Don Cockroft tied it at seventeen as the teams headed to the fourth quarter.

This is where things began to get crazy as first Brian Sipe and then Steve Grogan exchanged touchdown passes. Then, Cockroft and John Smith would exchange field goals to send the game into overtime at twenty-seven apiece. From there, another Cockroft field goal would win it for the Browns in walk-off fashion. The win sparked a 5–2 start, but eventually they would collapse, losing six of their final seven games, to finish 6–8 and miss the playoffs.

The 1979 season began on a high note for Cleveland as they started the season 3–0, as they welcomed in America's team in for Monday Night Football in a showcase of two of the NFL's most popular teams. The Browns were ready for the spotlight of National Prime Time television as they crushed the Dallas Cowboys 26–7 in a rout.

It was a wild start that saw the Browns leap out to a 20–0 lead. The Browns point barrage was courtesy of Sipe touchdown passes to Dave Logan and Ozzie Newsome. This was combined with a 39-yard interception touchdown return by Thom Darden off a Roger Staubach pass. Staubach would attempt to get them back in it with a 48-yard touchdown strike to Tony Hill by the time an explosive 20–7 first quarter was over.

Oddly enough, despite all the action in the opening quarter, the rest of the game would only see six more points in the closing seconds of the game as Greg Pruitt took it in from two yards out to cap the victory.

The win would move the Browns to 4–0; however, they would finish the season 5–5 and miss the playoffs once again.

As discussed in chapter 3, the Browns would win their only prime time game in the magical 1980 season against the Houston Oilers 16–7. All the fun of 1980 was evaporated week one of 1981 when they were blown out 44–14 at San Diego by the Chargers on Monday night to start the season.

The Browns returned to prime time in 1983 on a Thursday night as they hosted their in-state rival the Cincinnati Bengals. The NFL had seen the money-making ability and the popularity of Monday Night Football and decided to expand the schedule to Thursdays as well. Cleveland was one of the first franchises to be spotlighted on this platform and did well with it as they toppled the Bengals 17–7. The Orange and Brown had touchdowns from Ozzie Newsom and Mike Pruitt in the victory.

After a blowout 33–0 Monday Night Football loss to Seattle to open the 1984 season, the Browns bounced back with a 17–7 week 2 win over Pittsburgh in 1985. This was one of the final wins with Gary Danielson as the starting quarterback as the Bernie Kosar era would start a few short weeks after. On this night, however, it was the vaunted run game for Cleveland of Kevin Mack and Earnest Byner that combined for 120 yards on 30 carries. This was the 1985 season that saw both Mack and Byner run for 1,000 yards each.

When Miami rolled into Cleveland Municipal Stadium on Monday Night November 10, 1986, Browns fans only had one thing on their minds, and that was revenge. The Dolphins overcame a 21–3 deficit to the Browns the year prior in the playoffs to end Bernie Kosar's dream rookie season run. No one in Cleveland had forgotten about the second half heartbreak, and had this date with Miami circled on their schedule from the day it came out.

A packed house stood in anticipation of this showdown between Kosar and Dan Marino on prime time. Up 6–3 early into the second quarter, the Browns were the first to strike paydirt when little-known Harry Holt took one in from sixteen yards out to extend the lead to 16–6. The Dolphins answered back with a Marino to Mark Duper twenty-four-yard touchdown strike. Another field goal by Matt Bahr, his third of the first half, would extend the Browns lead to 16–10 at halftime.

The Browns went on to score two more times before the end of the night for an impressive 26–16 win. The incredible thing about this night on the shore was the fact that Bernie Kosar threw for 401 yards but not a single touchdown pass. Kevin Mack was held to just 27 yards on the ground, but went for 94 in the air, a career high!

The Browns used the momentum of that night to reach the AFC Championship game against Denver. The Browns were proving to be a force under the lights and showed it yet again as they defeated the Rams 30–17 at home midway through the 1987 season. Another year that ended in the AFC Championship game against Denver.

Headed into 1988, the Browns started to become the premier team of Monday and Thursday night football; this was never more evident than in 1988 when even without their banged-up starting quarterback Bernie Kosar, they defeated the Indianapolis Colts 23–17 with backup Mike Pagel. The backup shined in prime time, throwing for 255 yards and 2 touchdowns.

The 1989 season under Bud Carson was the last time the Browns reached the AFC Championship game, and it once again came with a Monday Night Football win. This time around it was NFC foe the Chicago Bears at home in Cleveland. The Browns stumbled out of the gate to a 3–3 record in 1989 and needed this win to get on the happy side of par.

They won easily with a 27–7 lopsided victory. The win would spark a four-game winning streak, and the Browns would eventually finish the season with a 9–5–1 mark, and once again reach the AFC Championship game versus Denver. In the win, Eric Metcalf rushed for a touchdown and received one as well. The big play came on a wild 97–yard touchdown toss to a wide-open Webster Slaughter from Bernie Kosar as the Browns led 24–0 at one point.

I mentioned another loss to Denver, but the following season in 1990, Monday Night Football would bring the opportunity to revenge that third loss in four years to the dreaded orange crush. The Broncos had made a habit of beating the Browns in the most heart-wrenching ways but this time around it was Cleveland sending Denver to bed with heartbreak.

Elway had thrown for 175 yards and also ran for a touchdown to help Denver build a 29–20 fourth quarter lead. This was combined with a 106 rushing yard night from Bobby Humphrey as it appeared that Denver would once again top Cleveland. This was when the Browns would begin to create their own fourth quarter magic.

It began with Bernie Kosar's third touchdown of the night as he threw for a total of 318 yards in the game. This was a 24-yard touchdown toss to Brian Brennan to keep hope alive as they suddenly only trailed 29–27 with minutes left in the game.

The Browns held John Elway and forced a rare Broncos punt that evening. Cleveland Browns placekicker Jerry Kauric who only played one year in the NFL had the chance to be a hero as Kosar moved the Browns into field goal position with only seconds left. It was then that Kauric trotted out there calmly nailed a thirty-yard kick as time expired to give the Browns the dramatic win. For Cleveland, it was their lone bright spot in what was a terrible 3–13 season that would lead to Bud Carson's dismissal as head coach during the bye week where the Browns sat 2–7 at the time.

The 1990 season saw a lot of pain for Cleveland fans, and a lot of setbacks as well. They wouldn't achieve their next prime time victory until nearly three years later when Bernie Kosar outdueled Steve Young, once again at home, to lead the Browns to a 23–13 victory.

The night truly proved to be historic as it would go down as the last time the Cleveland Browns won a game that Bernie Kosar started and played all four quarters in. The legendary and beloved quarterback of the Browns would be cut from the team by week 9 as head coach Bill Belichick cited Kosar as having "diminished skills." Belichick took a lot of heat for that move, but he was right to do it as it was clear that Kosar's days of being relevant had painfully come to an end.

This Monday night in Cleveland, however, belonged to Kosar and the Browns. Kosar outdueled Steve Young and the 49ers to the tune of 186 yards and a touchdown while the Browns secondary picked off Steve Young three times. It was Kosar's last great hurrah in Cleveland,

and would signal the end of many great times for Bernie since his arrival in 1985.

The Browns had to savor that win in 1993 because they would finish the season in turmoil 7–9 while missing the playoffs for a fourth straight year. As you read earlier the Browns would rebound well in 1994, going 11–5 and returning to the playoffs including a prime time win in week 7 against Houston to move to 5–1 on the season at that point.

Little did anyone realize that that win in October of 1994 against Houston would go down as the Browns' final win on prime time national television for the next nine years, as they wouldn't capture victory again on prime time until October of 2003. Now, to preface just a bit, they left the league after 1995 and didn't return until 1999. In the first four years they were back, they only had two prime time games, both losses on Sunday Night Football to Pittsburgh and Baltimore, and zero chance to play on Monday night.

As they entered this Sunday Night tilt against Pittsburgh on the road, they were reeling with a 1–3 start and their starting quarterback Kelly Holcomb was out due to injury. This brought the once–golden boy Tim Couch off the pine for a short redemption. He got exactly that with a sensational Sunday night performance over the Steelers who had knocked them out of the playoffs the previous winter.

Couch had the game of his life as he threw for two touchdowns and ran for one more in a dominant 33–13 Cleveland victory. He was helped out by a tremendous effort from the Browns defense who made the night for Steeler quarterback Tommy Maddox a living hell. The Browns defense picked off Maddox twice and sacked him three times. One of the interceptions resulted in a seventy-five-yard return for a touchdown from Daylon McCutcheon. Cleveland even doubled up Pittsburgh 22–11 in first downs that evening as well.

What was truly remarkable was the seventeen-year-long winless streak at Heinz Field that would develop after that. The Browns won that night at Heinz, and then not again until the 2020 playoff game at Heinz Field, which ironically enough, just happened to be on a Sunday night.

While the big win in Pittsburgh signaled the end of a nine-year drought it also began another one as the Browns wouldn't win again on prime time until five years later when they defeated the defending Super Bowl Champion New York Giants in Cleveland, on Monday night October 13, 2008, by a score of 35–14.

The win was huge for Cleveland as following a 10–6 season, all eyes were on the playoffs. They had underwhelmed by starting 0–3 to begin the season, and it looked like all that promise was going out the window. They managed a desperation win at hapless Cincinnati in week 4 to stop the losing streak, but few gave them a shot with the defending Super Bowl Champion New York Giants rolling into town.

Making matters worse were a couple of key factors working against Cleveland that night. The boo birds were already out during their first home game losses to Dallas and Pittsburgh to start the season. These same fans were calling for Romeo Crennel to replace Pro Bowl Quarterback Derek Anderson with second-year fan-favorite Brady Quinn out of Notre Dame. The pressure was on to prove that the 10–6 2007 season wasn't a fluke.

If the Browns were going to get things turned around, the odds were stacked against them as they would be playing without Kellen Winslow who was dealing with injury. At the time, Winslow was seen as one of the best tight ends in football and the Browns were hurting without him.

The Giants came in the defending Super Bowl Champions and even at only 4–0, the national media was already discussing the chances of them going 16–0. They were seen as almost unbeatable as their combined score through four weeks was 127–46. Coming into the Monday night showdown with Cleveland, Giants quarterback Eli Manning was throwing touchdown passes to Plaxico Burress and Amani Toomer left and right. Helping matters was the exciting combination in the backfield of power and speed that was Brandon Jacobs and Amad Bradshaw.

The defense was led by Justin Tuck and Antonio Pierce who made opposing quarterbacks shake in their cleats. The secondary of James Butler, Michael Johnson, Corey Webster, and Aaron Ross had opposing quarterbacks thinking twice every time they dropped back and scanned their routes. But just like they had done during so many previous Monday Night Games, the Cleveland Browns took the massive challenge head on, knowing that 80,000-plus screaming fans would be behind them.

The Browns knew that a 1–4 start to their season would spell death, but they were up for the challenge and appeared to be feeling no pressure, even after falling behind 7–3 early into the second quarter. Derek Anderson led back-to-back scoring drives, the first resulting in a Jamal Lewis four-yard touchdown run and the second on a twenty-two-yard touchdown pass to Darnell Dinkins. The Giants cut into the lead with a great two-minute drill that resulted in a Plaxico Burress touchdown catch.

Even with the Browns up 17–14 at the break, the national commentators still had a negative bias toward Cleveland and gave them little to no chance to hold onto the lead and win the game. The Browns were only able to add a field goal in the third quarter, but they did hold the Giants scoreless and held a slim 20–14 lead heading into the final fifteen minutes.

With all the pressure on their shoulders, the Browns didn't crumble; rather, they thrived to the tune of fifteen unanswered points to put the Giants away 35–14. The scoring was courtesy of an eleven-yard touchdown pass from Derek Anderson to Braylon Edwards. Then the cherry on the sundae came when Eric Wright intercepted an Eli Manning pass and took it ninety-four yards to the house for Cleveland!

It was a magical night in Cleveland, one that gave Browns fans hope. Derek Anderson lit up the Giants defense for 310 yards and 2 touchdown passes. His main target was Braylon Edwards who had 5 catches for 154 yards with the score and also a two-point conversion. Jamal Lewis rushed for 88 yards and a touchdown as well. The Browns defense stepped it up by picking off Eli Manning 3 times throughout the night.

Sadly, for Browns fans, the rest of the season was an epic disaster that never seemed to want to get better. They only won two more times, and ironically one of them was once again on a Monday night in Buffalo as a Phil Dawson 56-yard field goal into the wind, in the closing moments brought the Browns a 29–27 victory. It was part of a 5 field goal night for Dawson.

The 2009 season for the Cleveland Browns couldn't have started off any worse, as their record stood at a horrendous 1–11 as they headed into a Thursday night showcase game against the hated Pittsburgh Steelers. The Steelers came in at 6–6, and the Browns knew a win could knock

Pittsburgh out of playoff contention. That and the simple fact that this was a rivalry game being played in fifteen-degree weather with a wind of 25 mph that made it seem like –6 degrees out.

Ben Roethlisberger was a career 9–0 against Cleveland coming into this game and had little reason to fear the Browns. He was wrong not to take them seriously, as an angry Browns defense introduced him to the frozen turf all night long. The Browns sacked "Big Ben" a thunderous eight times throughout the course of the game. Those eight sacks resulted in sixty yards being lost and moving Pittsburgh out of field goal position time and time again.

On the opposite side of the spectrum, Browns quarterback Brady Quinn wasn't exactly a world beater, either, as he only went 6 of 19 for 90 yards. The crazy part of this Thursday night contest was the fact that Pittsburgh didn't score a single touchdown in the 13–6 Cleveland win, and the only person to score a touchdown was the never heard from before or again Browns tailback Chris Jennings who rushed for seventy-three yards. Another incredible stat was the one of Josh Cribbs, who made his bones as a kick and punt returner, rushing for a game high eighty-seven yards on jet sweeps and wildcat formations.

It wasn't pretty but it worked, and yet again the Browns were a prime time winner. A lot of fans believed it saved head coach Eric Mangini's job, as the Browns used that momentum from the stunning victory over the defending Super Bowl Champion Pittsburgh Steelers to win their final three games after that and completed the season at 5–11. It was also the second straight season the Browns defeated the defending Super Bowl Champions, they went on to make it the threepeat the next season with a victory of then-defending Super Bowl champion New Orleans.

It's almost a good thing that 2009 win was so "frozen," because the Browns had to keep it until they could replace it with another prime time win and that wouldn't happen for several years. In fact, the Browns' next big prime time nationally televised win wouldn't come until week 5 of the 2013 season, a little less than four full years later.

This win came over Buffalo and was steeped with drama coming into the night, and even more coming out of it. Once again, the Browns had stumbled out of the gate with an 0–2 record after poor losses to Miami at home and Baltimore on the road. A strange thing happened in the Baltimore game, however. After Browns second-year quarterback Brandon Weeden under-performed in the loss, he was injured and knocked out of the game late. Then his replacement, Jason Campbell, got dinged up while in relief, despite no one knowing until after.

Following the Browns 14–6 loss to Baltimore to start 0–2, two major changes happened. With both Weeden and Campbell hurt, they had to turn to third string quarterback and local product Brian Hoyer. The St. Ignatius graduate and Michigan State alumnus had spent three of his four seasons in the NFL learning underneath Tom Brady in New England. Hoyer was beloved in Cleveland from his time playing for Chuck Kyle at Saint Ignatius. Hoyer was a local product from a humble background and easy for Cleveland fans to get behind.

Coming into the week 3 game at Minnesota, Hoyer had thrown only sixty-seven passes in his NFL career. Not only was Hoyer without any experience, but also he would be without his number-one threat as the Browns shockingly and out of absolutely nowhere decided to trade away their stud running back Trent Richardson to the Indianapolis Colts. The Colts were looking for a running back after a season-ending injury to Vick Ballard.

The Browns selected Richardson in the first round with the third overall pick in the 2012 NFL Draft after they had traded picks with the Minnesota Vikings to select him ahead of the Tampa Bay Buccaneers. Richardson was the highest selected running back since Reggie Bush went second overall in 2006. Coming out of Alabama, he looked like a sure thing and would be the figurehead of the Browns turnaround as they went on to select quarterback Brandon Weeden later in the first round, and appeared to be headed to big numbers on offense with major weapons.

Richardson was one of the top high school prospects in the nation as he attended Escambia High School. As a junior, Richardson reached the 400-yard single game plateau, as he ran for 407 yards in his opening game against Tate High School. He finished his junior season (8 games) with 1,390 yards and 13 touchdowns, and received FSWA All-State 5A second team honors. He made the FSWA 5A All-State First Team as a senior, and was named 5A Florida Player of the Year and a finalist for the 2008 Mr. Football. Richardson also received consensus All-American honors and was named to the *Orlando Sentinel*'s All-Southern Team (Florida) his senior year when he ran for an incredible 2,100 yards on 228 carries scoring 25 touchdowns as a twelfth grader. In a game against Milton High School in September 2008, Richardson rushed for 419 yards on 29 carries and scored 6 touchdowns, a performance that earned him a selection as the first ESPN RISE National Football Player of the Week.

He was seen as a genetic freak on and off the field as he also excelled in other sports while at Escambia. Richardson lettered in track and field at Escambia. In 2008, he captured a regional title in the 100-meter dash (10.81 s) and placed fifth at the state meet with a time of 10.9 seconds. Considered a five-star recruit by *Rivals.com*, Richardson was listed as the No. 2 running back prospect in the nation when he committed to play for Nick Saban at Alabama.

He didn't wait long to prove he belonged at a big-name SEC school by answering the bell in big moments. Richardson was named SEC Freshman of the Week for week 2 when he had 118 rushing yards and two rushing touchdowns in the 40–14 victory over Florida International. Richardson was also named to the 2009 SEC All-Freshman team alongside Barrett Jones and Nico Johnson.

He caught the nation's eye in the 2010 BCS National Championship against the Texas Longhorns with 109 yards rushing and 2 touchdowns. All of this capped off a tremendous freshman season that saw him have 145 carries for 751 yards rushing and 8 touchdowns.

He was every bit as steady his sophomore year at Alabama as he had 12 carries for 700 yards rushing and 6 touchdowns and 266 yards receiving and 4 touchdowns. He did all of this while splitting carries with Mark Ingram, but once Ingram left for the NFL, Richardson's true talent began to show when he ran for over 100 yards in 9 games. He tied Shaun Alexander with 6 consecutive 100-yard rushing games. He scored 2 or more touchdowns in 7 games. He set a career-high against Ole Miss running for 183 yards and four touchdowns.

Once again, he saved his best for the brightest moments and biggest games as in the Iron Bowl game (season finale) against Auburn,

Richardson ran for a new career high of 203 yards in the 42–14 victory. In the 2012 BCS National Championship Game versus LSU, Richardson rushed for 96 yards and a touchdown to secure his second national championship with the Crimson Tide.

His senior season was another chance to capture plenty of hardware as well. He won the Doak Walker Award, becoming the first player from Alabama to win. He finished third in the Heisman Trophy, voting behind eventual winner Robert Griffin III and Andrew Luck—ironically, the same two players to be drafted ahead of him in the 2012 NFL Draft. All of this finished off a brilliant junior season that saw Richardson have 1,679 rushing yards, breaking Mark Ingram II's record for most rushing yards in a season, and 21 rushing touchdowns. His 21 rushing touchdowns was also an SEC running back record. His Alabama career finished with a total of 3,130 yards with 35 touchdowns on the ground.

When the Browns selected him third overall, it truly seemed like a sure thing. Browns fans would have to wait to see him on the field, however, as on August 9, 2012, Richardson underwent arthroscopic surgery to remove some cartilage fragments in his left knee. This forced him to miss the entire preseason, but he was to return in time for the season opener. Then opening week against the Philadelphia Eagles at home, with the anticipation to watch him play sky high, he came out and laid an egg as he was stifled to only 39 yards on 19 carries in a Cleveland Browns loss.

Richardson bounced back from the week 1 laid egg to finish his rookie season with 950 yards in 15 games on 267 attempts with 9 touchdowns. He also caught 51 balls for 267 yards and 1 touchdown. He was the first Browns rookie to rush for over 100 yards and score rushing and receiving touchdowns in the same game. During week 13, against the Kansas City Chiefs, Richardson rushed for 42 yards and 2 touchdowns, tying Jim Brown's franchise rookie record of 9 touchdowns.

Speaking of Jim Brown, the grizzled legend was not impressed with Richardson and openly criticized him in the media by calling the Browns rookie "average." It was hard to argue with Brown as Richardson rushed for 3.6 yards per carry, which was the lowest yards per carry stat for a rookie running back in the NFL 2012 season. While the actions of Jim

Brown were extremely questionable off the field, he knew his football and had Richardson pegged.

Still, for the Browns, they needed a threat like Richardson because they had no idea what they were going to get from Brian Hoyer. Browns general manager Tom Heckert didn't hesitate to pull the trigger on Richardson. He decided to ride and die with veteran running back Will McGahee who was in his eleventh and final year in the NFL after a decent career with the Denver Broncos, Buffalo Bills, and Baltimore Ravens.

McGahee was known for missing his entire rookie year in Buffalo after a gruesome leg injury sustained in the 2003 National Championship Game against Ohio State while playing for The University of Miami, Florida. In the early part of the fourth quarter during the 2003 Fiesta Bowl National Championship Game, McGahee suffered an injury after catching a screen pass from Dorsey. He was immediately hit by Buckeye safety Will Allen, bending his left knee backward and causing tears of the ACL, PCL, and MCL.

Prior to getting hurt, he had rushed for sixty-seven yards and a touchdown, as Miami would lose the game in double-overtime, 31–24. This injury required several surgeries and extensive rehabilitation before he would be able to play again. At the season's end, McGahee announced he would not collect on a $2.5 million insurance policy he had taken out before the championship game, and therefore would enter the 2003 NFL Draft.

He had a remarkable career at Miami, winning one national championship and finishing fourth in the Heisman Trophy balloting in 2002. He had rushed for 2,067 yards and 31 touchdowns in his college career when he was selected with the twenty-third overall pick in the 2003 NFL Draft by the Buffalo Bills. Prior to his knee injury in the 2003 Fiesta Bowl, McGahee was considered "a cinch top-five pick." By the time he showed up in Cleveland, his career was pretty much done—and it wasn't a bad one either, that saw him reach the 1,000-yard plateau three times, and also 990 yards in 2006. He was a serviceable back, but he wasn't the young stud Browns fans thought Richardson would be.

Down to their third string quarterback, the Browns were in a hole and a lot of people thought perhaps they were tanking the season to have a shot at taking Texas A&M quarterback Johnny Manziel in the early part of the 2014 NFL Draft. Well, those fans would get their wish, but it would lead to a series of events no one could have predicted—but more on that later.

As the Browns prepared for the Vikings with very little firepower, they did have some good news with at least one stealth weapon coming back in the form of second year wideout Josh Gordon. He was a standout in his rookie season, catching balls from Brandon Weeden all 16 games, as he finished his rookie campaign with 805 yards on 50 receptions with 5 touchdowns.

Gordon, Weeden, and Richardson were seen as the future of the Cleveland Browns and a reason for fans to dream of 40–50-point games being a regular thing by the offense. Now, two games into their sophomore seasons, Richardson was traded away, Weeden appeared to be a bust sitting on the bench nursing an injury, and Gordon was suspended for the first two games of the 2013 season. Why was he suspended? Well, let's back up a few steps.

Josh Gordon was a physical specimen and a three-sport all-star at Lamar High School in Houston where he excelled at track, football, and basketball. He ran a leg on the Lamar 4 × 100m and 4 × 200m relay squads, helping them capture the state title in both events with times of 42.69 seconds and 1:30.43 minutes, respectively. Football was no exception to his success, just addition; as a senior, he was named first-team All-District 20–5A after totaling 25 receptions for 531 yards (21.2 average) and 9 touchdowns.

With his natural skill, he should have had the choice to play his college ball wherever he wanted; however, due to substance abuse issues and legal problems, he was limited to playing in Texas only. Gordon accepted an athletic scholarship to play football for Baylor University. Although he received multiple Division I offers, his choice of Baylor was easy due to his supervised probation which required him not to leave the state of Texas. In October 2010, during his sophomore year, he and teammate Willie Jefferson were found asleep in a local Taco

Bell drive-through lane. Police found marijuana in Jefferson's car. Jefferson, who was driving, was kicked off the team due to it being his second violation, but Gordon was only suspended.

Gordon didn't learn from his mistakes and failed to properly take advantage of a third chance when, in July 2011, Gordon was suspended indefinitely by head coach Art Briles for later failing a drug test and testing positive for marijuana. His Baylor career lasted all of two seasons and when he arrived at Utah, it was too late; thus those two years as a Baylor Bear were the only NCAA action he saw.

Cleveland was desperate for talent on the skill positions, any talent no matter their history, and went after Gordon. He was taken in the second round of the 2012 Supplemental Draft by the Cleveland Browns. After a trouble-free rookie season, Gordon was back to his old devilish ways by the summer following his rookie season when, on June 7, 2013, the NFL announced that Gordon would be suspended for the first two games of the 2013 season due to violating the NFL's substance-abuse policy.

He would be back for week 3 to help Brian Hoyer as they traveled to take on the 0–2 Minnesota Vikings. Their 0–2 was a bit different than the Browns, however, as they had lost both of their games by a combined eight points and led late in the fourth quarter of both. The Vikings easily could have been 2–0 coming into the week 3 clash.

The game was stunning as Browns head coach Rob Chudzinski dialed up a game plan of almost all passing. McGahee only ran the ball 8 times as Brian Hoyer completed 30 of 54 passing for 321 yards in stunning fashion. Hoyer and Gordon had instant chemistry as Gordon went off for 10 catches on 19 targets for 146 yards, including a first quarter 47-yard touchdown bomb in the Browns 31–27 victory. Perhaps the only drawback may have been Hoyer forcing the ball to Gordon a bit, as he was picked off three times throughout the game. The interceptions were a small price to pay for a major road win that even included a thrilling last-second touchdown pass to tight end Jordan Cameron to win it.

Suddenly Cleveland had Hoyer fever as the hometown kid appeared to be the savior. Hysteria reached an all-time high following the week 4 victory over Cincinnati at home in a game that featured two more touchdown passes from Hoyer and 269 passing yards!

Hoyer was the man and his connection with Gordon appeared to be deadly. Now it was time to show it off on prime time as Thursday Night Football came to town for their week 5 home game versus Buffalo. Another packed crowd filed into Cleveland Browns First Energy Stadium for a prime time showdown with a long-time AFC rival.

The first quarter went very badly for Cleveland as they dug themselves a quick 10–0 hole. Making matters even worse was Brian Hoyer getting knocked out of the game due to getting hit while sliding and tearing his ACL. Suddenly, all that hope, all that hype for Hoyer, was over just like that!

Chudzinski had no choice but to go to the bench and put in the now healthy Brandon Weeden who was just chomping at the bit for a second chance. A little-known fact about Weeden was that he was twenty-nine years old when he was drafted because he didn't start his college football career until his late twenties. His first love and passion was baseball and he almost had a pro career as a pitcher.

Weeden was drafted in the second round of the 2002 Major League Baseball Draft by the New York Yankees as their first selection in the draft. After the 2003 season, he was traded to the Los Angeles Dodgers with Jeff Weaver and Yhency Brazobán for Kevin Brown. Following the 2005 season, he was selected in the Rule 5 draft by the Kansas City Royals. Weeden played his last season of professional baseball in 2006 for the Class-A High Desert Mavericks of the California League. Injuries and poor performance led Weeden to quit baseball.

Weeden, as mentioned, was the twenty-second pick in the quarterback-heavy 2012 NFL Draft that also featured Robert (RG3) Griffith, Andrew Luck, and Ryan Tannehill selected before him. His rookie season had its ups and down, including one of the worst NFL debuts in history as Weeden was named starter week 1 of the 2012 season in which he had a 5.1 passer rating after throwing four interceptions in a loss to the Philadelphia Eagles, which is the sixth lowest in a season opener by any quarterback attempting at least fifteen passes since the merger in 1970.

It wasn't easy for Weeden to begin with because fans loved Colt McCoy whom he replaced without even having a quarterback competition in preseason. Weeden would go on to have a mediocre rookie season with only 14 touchdowns in 15 starts, compared to 17 interceptions. He also fumbled 6 times in the 28 times he was sacked. That was perhaps his biggest flaw; he was seen as a turnover machine.

Down 10–0 to Buffalo, the Browns didn't need rookie season Brandon Weeden, they needed the guy who lit it up for the Oklahoma State Cowboys. In his senior season, 2011, he led Oklahoma State to an 11–1 regular season, a number 3 ranking in the BCS standings, and a berth in the 2012 BCS Tostitos Fiesta Bowl. He also broke school records in total attempts, completions, yardage, and touchdowns. In 12 games, Weeden completed 379 of 522 passes for 4,328 yards. He saved his best for last as in the 2012 Fiesta Bowl, he threw for 399 yards, completed 29 of 42 passes, and had 4 touchdowns in a 41–38 win against the Stanford Cardinals.

Weeden set numerous records for passing, and offensive performance at Oklahoma State University including 4,727 passing yards in the 2011 season. Honors included being named a 2010 All-Big 12 Quarterback, First-team. He was also a 2010 Manning Award Finalist.

He had the pedigree and raw talent, but coming into a pro–Brian Hoyer crowd, down 10–0, he was going to need the heart! Like a scene out of a Disney movie, the Browns outscored the Bills 17–0 in the second quarter to take the halftime lead 17–14. A field goal by Bully Cundiff and touchdown run by McGahee would tie it at 10, and then a 79-yard punt return by Travis Benjamin right before halftime gave them the lead.

After consecutive Buffalo rushing touchdowns made it 24–17 deep into the third quarter, Weeden tied it up once again when he hooked up with Josh Gordon for 37-yard touchdown to make it 24 all headed into the fourth quarter.

Two Billy Cundiff field goals gave the Browns a slim 30–24 late in the game. The Bills had the ball with two minutes to go and quarterback Jeff Tuel was starting to put together a game-winning drive for the Bills as Browns fans slumped in their seats with the thought "same old Browns" going through their heads. It was then that the vaunted

Cleveland Browns magic struck on prime time once again, when safety T. J. Ward picked off a Tuel pass and returned it for a 44-yard touchdown to put the game away while helping the Browns improve to 3–2.

Brandon Weeden got the relief win, but didn't exactly light the world on fire as he was sacked five more times, fumbling once and only throwing for 197 yards. However, the Thursday Night NFL Network crew went into full hype mode afterward as Weeden sat on their set and Deon Sanders rained praise on Weeden, calling him the future of the Cleveland Browns. He went as far as to crown Weeden the full-time starter.

It was comical as clearly the Browns didn't listen and he was gone by the following summer. The big night couldn't help Weeden in the long term, however, as he finished the season with a stat line of 9 touchdowns, 9 interceptions, and only 1,731 yards as he would eventually get replaced once again by Jason Campbell.

With Trent Richardson gone, and Brandon Weeden officially a bust, the true superstar and future of the Cleveland Browns in 2013 was Josh Gordon. The second-year sensation had a career year that would prove to do nothing more than tease Browns fans with what "could have been." Gordon was untouchable in 2013 as he finished the 2013 season with a league-leading 1,646 receiving yards and was named a first-team All-Pro. In Week 12, Gordon had 237 receiving yards, and 261 the following week, the first time in NFL history that a wide receiver had back-to-back regular season games with at least 200 receiving yards. He was named the Cleveland Chapter PFWA Player of the Year following the season.

Headed into the 2014 season, a healthy Brian Hoyer and a returning Josh Gordon had fans dreaming of an AFC North Championship. They just didn't need any distractions and the Browns could have done some serious damage in the AFC. Sadly, Gordon couldn't stay clean and the Browns drafted two gigantic distractions in the opening round of the 2014 NFL Draft.

On July 5, 2014, Gordon was arrested for driving while impaired in Raleigh, North Carolina. A few weeks later the NFL suspended him for one year for violating the league's substance-abuse policy. On September 19, 2014, his suspension was reduced to ten games amid the new NFL drug policy.

What really hurt the Browns was the debacle of an NFL Draft they had in May of 2014. With the thought that they had a stud at wide receiver with Gordon, and the signing of free agent Miles Austin from the Dallas Cowboys, the Browns elected to pass on drafting 5-star wideouts Sammy Watkins, Mike Evans, Odell Beckham Jr., and Brandin Cooks.

Instead, they opted to draft defensive back Justin Gilbert out of Oklahoma Stat with the eighth overall pick and Johnny Manziel, quarterback out of Texas A&M with the twenty-second overall pick. Gilbert and Manziel would do battle all season long to compete as to who was the bigger bust.

The Gilbert bust was shocking as he won the 2013 College Football Performance Award as the nation's top defensive back. The Browns were hoping to line him up with Joe Haden and create a lights out secondary like they had with Frank Minniefield and Handford Dixon in the 1980s. It was not to be, however, as Gilbert got burned more times than a flame thrower at the circus. It didn't help matters that he missed several team meetings and practices because he couldn't get out of bed after staying up all night playing video games.

It wasn't just defense stops they needed Gilbert for, but they were counting on him to spark a return game that had been dead since Josh Cribbs left. Gilbert, as a senior in 2013, set the Big 12 Conference record for kickoff return touchdowns with six. Again, it was not to be as he was a total bust and played his way out of Cleveland by the start of the 2016 season.

The true disaster of the 2014 draft was the fact that the Browns traded up with Dallas to select Johnny Manziel, aka Johnny Football, aka Johnny Manziel—aka total train wreck! Never had a Heisman Trophy come into the NFL with the hype that Manziel had around him. The only ones I could compare him to as far as hype went were Desmond Howard and Tim Tebow. The difference with those guys however was even though their careers were a bust, at least they worked hard, met with some success, had heart, and were great teammates. Manziel was none of that!

It was clear that Brian Hoyer was not the first choice of Cleveland Browns owner Jimmy Haslam and overstepped his General Manager Ray Farmer by forcing him to select Manziel even though all of their scouring reports said stay away, and draft either Derek Carr or Teddy Bridgewater who were both there at twenty-two.

You almost couldn't blame Haslam for buying into the hype as Manziel had a ton of it coming into the NFL Draft process. It started in high school as he became a Texas high school football legend at Tivy High School. His stats and charisma are the making of folklore legend!

His junior year was his first as starting quarterback, and he completed that season with 2,903 passing yards, 1,544 rushing yards, 152 receiving yards, and 55 touchdowns. That year, he was voted All-San Antonio Area Offensive Player of the Year as well as District 27–4A MVP. He was just getting started!

During Manziel's senior season, he compiled 228-of-347 (65.7%) passing for 3,609 yards with 45 touchdowns and five interceptions. He also had 170 carries for 1,674 yards and 30 touchdowns. He had one touchdown reception and returned a kickoff for a touchdown for a combined 77 touchdowns. That year, he was honored as District 28–4A MVP (unanimous selection), Class 4A First-team All-State (AP), *San Antonio Express-News* Offensive Player of the Year (second year in a row), the Associated Press Sports Editors Texas Player of the Year, Sub-5A First-team All-Area (*SA Express-News*), No. 1 QB in Texas by *Dave Campbell's Texas Football*, DCTF Top 300, PrepStar All-Region and Super-Prep All-Region.

By the time his run at Tivy was over, he completed 520-of-819 passes (63.5%) for 7,626 yards and 76 touchdowns, rushed 531 times for 4,045 yards and 77 touchdowns, and caught 30 passes for 582 yards and another 5 touchdowns. He was the only quarterback in America named as a Parade All-American his senior year, and he was also named the National High School Coaches Association (NHSCA) Senior Athlete of the Year in football. To the shock of no one, he won the 2010 Mr. Texas Football Award.

When you're a standout at high school football in Texas, you never pay for a meal again in your hometown! The problem for Manziel is that fame can often come with temptation and a tendency to get in trouble. He found it before he could take a single snap for Texas A&M. On June 29, 2012—before his first college game—Manziel was arrested and charged with three misdemeanors—disorderly conduct, failure to produce identification, and possession of a fictitious driver's license. These charges stemmed from a late-night fight in College Station, Texas. In July 2013, he pleaded guilty to failure to produce identification, and the other two charges were dismissed.

Police reports stated that Manziel was with a friend who directed a racial slur at a man on the street. The man then approached the two of them and tried to get at the friend, but Manziel placed himself between the two men, saying his friend didn't mean it and he was going to take him home. The man continued pushing against Manziel to reach the other man, and Manziel eventually pushed back.

At this point, the man swung at Manziel who then began fighting back. Shortly afterward, the bicycle patrol officers arrived. Manziel was nineteen at the time, and he presented to police officers a fake Louisiana driver's license that showed him to be twenty-one years of age. Manziel was taken into custody and reportedly spent the night in jail.

On August 4, 2013, ESPN reported that the NCAA was investigating whether Manziel accepted payments for autographs that he had signed in January 2013. The NCAA did not find any evidence that Manziel accepted money for the autographs, but reached an agreement with Texas A&M to suspend him for the first half of the season opener against Rice University, due to an "inadvertent violation" of NCAA rules. He continued to get free passes when he should have been punished time and time again. It was setting him up for disaster.

Jimmy Haslam looked past all of that, and focused on what he did while on the field at A&M instead, which was also the stuff of legend. He set the following records that once seemed impossible to pass until he showed up:

- Freshman record: rushing yards by a quarterback, season (1,410)
- Freshman record: total offense, season (5,116)

- Tenth-most (at the time) single-season total offensive yards in NCAA FBS history
- Most games with 300 or more passing yards and 100+ rushing yards, career (4)
- First freshman (and fifth player ever) in FBS history with 3,000 passing yards and 1,000 rushing yards in a season
- FBS record: Rushing yards by a quarterback in a bowl game (229 yards)
- Only the fourth player to have 20 passing TDs and 20 rushing TDs, season
- Eclipsed the 7,000-yard barrier in total offense in his nineteenth career game, which is the fastest in NCAA FBS history by a four-year player
- Second freshman in FBS history to rush for 1,000 yards and pass for 2,000 yards
- First freshman to win the Heisman Trophy
- First freshman to win the Davey O'Brien National Quarterback Award
- First freshman to win the Manning Award
- 2012 Heisman Trophy winner (first freshman to win)
- 2012 Davey O'Brien National Quarterback Award winner (first freshman to win)
- 2012 Manning Award winner (first freshman to win)
- 2012 Sporting News College Football Player of the Year
- 2012 SEC Offensive Player of the Year
- 2012 SEC Freshman of the Year
- 2012 All-SEC First-team Quarterback
- 2013 Cotton Bowl Classic—Offensive MVP
- 2013 Chick-fil-A Bowl—Offensive MVP

But for Manziel, it wasn't just the awards and record that made him beloved by fans and coveted by owners, it was his winning spirit and uncanny ability to win the big game against all odds. In fact, he had some of his biggest games against Texas A&M's biggest rivals. Three of his best performances came against Arkansas, Alabama, and Auburn in the SEC.

He holds the record for Texas A&M passing yards in a game. He owns the top three spots, as matter of fact, as he balled out against the SEC's best. In his first 10 games, Manziel had 4 of the top 10 games in total offense in Texas A&M history. He logged 10 straight games with 300 or more total yards, 21 total games with 300+ yards.

His top 3 performances as an Aggie were:

- 464 yards against No. 1 Alabama on September 14, 2013,
- 454 yards against Auburn on October 19, 2013, and
- 453 yards against Arkansas on September 29, 2012.

With all that being said, even though Hoyer looked to be the man and the Browns badly needed help in other areas, Haslam overrode Ray Farmer, and "Money Manziel" was headed to Cleveland.

Even with the gigantic distractions that the Gordon drug suspension caused and the Manziel drama that seemed to be in the press every single day with something stupid, including him flicking off opposing fans during a preseason game in Washington. On August 22, 2014, Manziel was fined $12,000 by the NFL for a hand gesture that he made in the preseason loss. First year head coach Mike Pettine had seen enough and named fellow quarterback Brian Hoyer the starter over Manziel for the opening regular season.

Like the 2007 Cleveland Browns that won ten games, the 2014 Cleveland Browns also lost their opening game to Pittsburgh before beginning a solid run to contend for an AFC North Crown. The Browns bounced back from heartbreaking losses to Pittsburgh and Baltimore to start the season 5–3 and looked impressive doing it. Through those first eight games, Hoyer threw for over 2,000 yards, nearly double-digit touchdowns and had the Browns contending. The run included a twenty-one-point fourth quarter rally to beat Tennessee on the road, and a blowout victory over Pittsburgh.

The "Johnny Johnny" chants had almost completely died down, and Hoyer was the man when Cleveland headed to Cincinnati for a Thursday night showdown. The Bengals had also started the season 5–2–1 at the midseason mark and many felt were looking right past Cleveland to future matchups with Pittsburgh and Baltimore. They didn't take the Browns and Brian Hoyer seriously and they paid for it as it was all Orange and Brown in a 24–3 blowout!

The Browns held Bengals quarterback Andy Dalton to a humiliating 10 of 33 passing for a paltry 86 yards and 3 interceptions. The Browns defense was a thing of beauty, even if Justin Gilbert had nothing to do with it. The three-headed rushing monster of Terrence West, Isiah Crowell, and Ben Tate combined for 170 yards on the ground. The stout running game took the pressure off of Hoyer who went 15 of 23 for 198 yards.

In what could only be described as irony was that this game took place on a Thursday night in front of the same crew that saw Weeden replace Hoyer for a big victory the year before. This time around it was Deion Sanders heaping praise on Hoyer and stating that it should be him and not Manziel getting the big money from the Browns and a long-term contract. The irony of the comments from Sanders were off the page!

Hoyer had the Browns at 6–3 after that impressive Thursday night win, but Ray Farmer, Jimmy Haslam, and Mike Pettine couldn't resist the Manziel hype too much later and Hoyer was benched by week 13 with the Browns at 7–6 and still in contention. Manziel would take the team and season right down the toilet when he decided partying with Josh Gordon was more important than showing up to the game on time and also knowing any of the playbook.

The Browns would finish 7–9 and Josh Gordon was suspended again before the season could even finish. On December 27, 2014, exactly one year removed from being selected into the Pro Bowl, the Browns suspended Gordon from the final game of the season due to a violation of team rules. The violation was that he and Manziel decided to get together and have some drug-alcohol mix called "purple drank."

It wasn't much longer until Gordon was suspended for the entire 2015 season due to violating the league's substance abuse policy. Gordon entered the NFL's substance abuse program after pleading guilty to a driving while impaired charge in September 2014 and was prohibited from consuming alcohol during his time in the program. The suspension was for one year starting on February 3, 2015, and he was not eligible to return until the start of the 2016 season.

Following the 2015 season, his request to be reinstated was denied in March when it was reported that he had failed another drug test. It simply wasn't meant to be for Gordon in Cleveland, or anywhere else for that matter as the rest of his career was marred by drug issues.

That 2014 NFL Draft messed the Browns up so badly that they wouldn't start winning prime time games again until Baker Mayfield showed up in 2018 and they seemed to get games on either Monday night, Thursday night, Saturday night, or Sunday on a regular basis.

A few of those highlights include Baker's regular season debut in 2018 versus the New York Jets on a Thursday night with color rush jerseys. The 2018 victory at Denver on a Sunday night that moved the Browns to 6–7–1 and gave them an outside chance at the playoffs.

## 2019 SEASON WEEK TWO AT NEW YORK JETS
### Cleveland 23, Jets 3
How ironic is it that Jets' defensive coordinator Gregg Williams took a sick pride in hurting players to the point where their careers are put in jeopardy, and this night, it was his team's QB violently knocked from the game by Myles Garrett ending what little chance the Jets had in this one.

The Browns didn't look great by any stretch, 9 more penalties for 85 yards and sloppy play at times, but all that aside, they happily took the 23–3 victory and moved forward with their season.

As mentioned, the Browns and Garrett knocked Jets starting quarterback Trevor Siemian from the game in the second quarter with several violent hits. Garrett was a game changer with three sacks and took residence in the Jets backfield all evening.

Simian wasn't exactly lighting the world on fire to that point, only tossing for 3 yards on 3 of 6 passing, getting sacked twice. His replacement Luke Faulk went 20 for 25 for 198 yards but never really led a touchdown-threatening drive.

The only threat the Jets had left was LeVeon Bell, who was held in check by a hungry Browns D-line. Bell was throttled and held to 68 yards on 21 carries. He did have 61 yards on 10 catches as well, but the Browns defensive held him in check and kept him from changing the game.

The Browns defense was the story of the night in many ways, keeping pressure on the quarterbacks all night long and holding New York to only 262 total yards. The Browns also held the Jets to 2 of 12 on third down, keeping the Browns' defense fresh and ready to go.

On the fun side of the ball, the Browns finally gave fans what they had been thirsting for since they traded for Odell Beckham Jr. the prior spring. OBJ went off for 161 yards on 6 catches, including an 89-yard catch and run from Baker Mayfield at the tail end of the third quarter to put the game away. That touchdown was the only points scored in a clunky second half.

For Baker, it was part of a 325-yard night that saw him get sacked and picked off once. His touchdown pass to OBJ was his only one of the night, and one of only two touchdowns scored during the entire game.

The other touchdown was scored by Nick Chubb at the 10:16 mark of the second. Chubb burst through a Jets blitz to score from 19 yards out and extend the Browns lead to 13–0. For Chubb, it was part of a 62 rushing yard night, along with 4 catches for 36 yards.

The Jets cut into the 13–0 lead with a field goal midway through the second quarter by Sam Ficken. Anyone who didn't know who Sam Ficken was before the game started, the announcers spent a good fifteen minutes telling the fans all about him as if he was the second coming of Morten Anderson.

The Browns would tack on three more in the closing moments of the half, as Austin Seibert would convert a field goal from 43 yards to make it 16–3 at the half. Siebert had a good night, converting 3 of 3 in the field goal game, making them from 23, 48, and 43 yards.

## 2022 SEASON WEEK 8
### Cleveland 32, Cincinnati 13

The Cleveland Browns hosted the Cincinnati Bengals in a "Win or your season is over" type game Halloween night. After starting out the season a promising 2–1 with a Thursday night prime time win over their rivals the Pittsburgh Steelers, they dropped four straight games in agonizing fashion to the Baltimore Ravens, New England Patriots, Atlanta Falcons, and Los Angeles Chargers.

The most painful part of all of that was with the sole exception of the Patriots game, when the Browns had the ball in their hands with a chance to win the game in the final seconds.

The same could be said for their week 2 loss against the New York Jets. Each time, they had a chance to win when the clock struck 00:00. They would leave nothing to chance on this night, however, with a commanding and dominant total team win over the Bengals by a score of 32–13.

After the first twenty-five minutes of the game proved to be a defensive lockdown as both teams failed to score, the Browns broke through with their stud back Nick Chubb on a three-yard rush. They moved quarterback Jacoby Brissett out wide and slid Chubb into a Wildcat formation, as well as bringing in two extra offensive linemen.

The score came with 5:07 left in the half. Following the touchdown the Bengals jumped offsides on the ensuing extra point, so Browns Head Coach Kevin Stefanski decided to go for two points, which Chubb cashed in on again to make it 8–0. The Browns would add a 55-yard Cade York field goal to take an 11–0 lead into the second half.

The second half was all Browns as they scored on their first three possessions to put the game out of reach 32–6 about halfway through the third quarter, thanks in part to touchdown runs from Chubb and Brissett along with a four-yard touchdown pass to Amari Cooper.

On the night Nick Chubb ran for 101 yards on 23 carries with 2 scores, Brissett went 17 of 22 passing with a pick and a touchdown toss to Cooper. The win improved the Browns record to 3–5 on the season heading into a bye week, and only three more games until the debut of suspended quarterback Deshaun Watson.

One thing is for sure, from that Monday night in 1970 through the games played in 2022, the Browns bring it in prime time. It could be the NFL Network on a Thursday or Hank Williams Junior on a Monday night, the Browns fans are ready for some football!

# CHAPTER 7

# Bright Stars During Dark Times

No Browns fan on planet Earth can dispute the fact that the stretch between the ending of the 2007 season in which they went 10–6, and the 2020 season when they returned to the playoffs by beating the Pittsburgh Steelers, and then on top of that, beat their rivals at Heinz Field to win their first playoff game since 1994, was the worst stretch in Cleveland football history. The list of things that went horribly wrong in that twelve-year stretch between 2008–2019 is just too hard to live through again by listing.

Instead of going down that path one more time, I wanted to shed some light on a list of players who gave Cleveland Browns fans at least some small reason to tune in while the Browns went 51–140–1 from the start of the 2008 season through the end of the 2019 season. They literally won 26 percent of their games which is roughly four wins a season. It doesn't get much more painful than that as they only reached seven wins twice during that stretch, won zero season openers, and had seasons of 0, 1, and 4 victories.

Despite all of that, the following players for the following reasons, kept us tuning in and cheering. They kept jersey sales up and gave everyone wearing Orange and Brown at least a little room to puff out their chests.

I'm going to start by covering a few players who were already on the team when that dark period started, including three of them who either experienced the playoffs or a ten-win season at some point. The first is Phil Dawson. He was with Cleveland from day one of their rebirth as the Browns signed him as a free agent in March 1999, and he remained with the team for fourteen years until he joined the San Francisco 49ers in 2013. The franchise tagged him several times before 2013 as he was one of the fist kickers that was often seen as the most valuable player on the team. How many times can you say that about a placekicker?

Dawson actually went to the same high school as Cleveland Browns legendary place kicker Matt Strover. Years apart of course, but they both attended Lake Highlands High School in Dallas, Texas. As a senior, he was a starter at both kicker and offensive tackle until he hurt his knee in a preseason scrimmage. He bounced back from the injury and was named as an All-American and the Southwest Region Offensive Player of the Year by SuperPrep.

His high school career was good enough to land a scholarship offer to play for Mac Brown at the University of Texas where he continued to excel. While in Austin, he was a four-year letterman in football. After redshirting his freshman year, he scored eighty points his first year of playing. He also tied a school record with fifty-four consecutive extra points.

The following season, he made honorary All-America honors while leading the Longhorns in scoring. He made first-team All-America his junior and senior years, while simultaneously making All-Big 12. He earned a BA in political science.

In what can only be described as a giant bit of irony, he showed everyone that he could kick in bad weather as he would spend the majority of his career in it as well, despite no one thinking about Big 12 football as bad weather but he proved it. In 1995 he kicked game-winning field goal against the University of Virginia, booting a 50-yarder against a 30 mph wind to give Texas a thrilling 17–16 victory as time expired. He showed everyone watching that weather wouldn't matter—he had nerves of steel.

After failed attempts to make the Oakland Raiders and New England Patriots in the 1998 season, he landed in Northeast Ohio, which would become his home. After winning a narrow kicking battle in training camp for the Browns, he was given a chance to start and play in his first NFL game on opening night for the Browns as they hosted Pittsburgh. Sadly, Dawson never saw the field once all night as the

Browns only kickoff was by their punter Chris Gardocki who was their designated kickoff kicker. The Browns never scored a single point or even sniffed field goal range in the disastrous 43–0 opening night loss.

Thus, Dawson's first career points came the following week in Tennessee as he kicked a -41-yard field goal to give the Browns their first points in their new franchise's history in a 26–9 loss. It was one of several firsts that year for Dawson; on October 10 of that season, he scored the only touchdown of his career on a fake field goal against the Bengals in an 18–17 loss.

It came on a trick play as Chris Gardocki the holder flipped him the ball and Dawson scrambled in for the four-yard touchdown rush. It gave the Browns the lead and they managed to hold onto it until Cincinnati scored on a touchdown pass from Akili Smith to Carl Pickens with five seconds left to break everyone's hearts and hand the Bengals the win.

Perhaps Dawson's greatest memory of the first season as a Cleveland Brown came in week 10 when he made his first-ever game winner against Pittsburgh at Three Rivers to help the Browns win 16–15 in dramatic fashion. The kick was good from thirty-nine yards out as time expired.

It was the first of many big performances for the two-time second team All-Pro and the 2012 Pro Bowler. The following season in 2000, he would hit another game winner over Pittsburgh, this time at home from nineteen yards to win it for Cleveland. In 2001 at Tennessee, he hit a clutch 44-yard field goal to give the Browns a last-second 41–38 victory.

The following season in 2002, Dawson would do it again in Tennessee, this time in overtime with a 33-yard kick to cap off a thrilling 28–14 comeback for the 31–28 win. Dawson would do it to the Jets later that same season with a 35-yard field goal to win it 24–21 over the Jets.

We told you about his thrilling double doink against Baltimore during the magical 2007 season, but he also had big moments in many other games, such as on November 17, 2008, when Dawson hit a fifty-six-yard game-winning field goal against the Buffalo Bills on Monday Night Football. In a game where the Browns' season was already over and they had nothing to play for, Dawson gave fans a reason to smile!

In 2010, the 4–7 Browns were tied with the Miami Dolphins on the road, as Dawson nailed a twenty-three-yard field goal to win the game 13–10 and give the Browns their fifth and final win of the 2010 season.

All of this was something beautiful as he scored 1,265 points in thirteen seasons with the Browns. No one else even comes close to a fraction of that point total. Dawson was a sure thing from inside of fifty yards kicking in the toughest stadium in all of football to kick. For his career with Cleveland, he went 305 of 363 for an outstanding 84 percent. He was a sure thing for the Browns time and time again, when many things weren't.

Since 2013 and his departure, the Browns have gone through one place kicker after another with none panning out. Twice they used draft picks on kickers to no avail as neither Austin Seibart in 2019 or Cade York in 2022 worked out.

Everyone blamed a bad offensive line for the failures of Tim Couch. By the time 2007 rolled around, the O-Line still hadn't been one of the best in football, and that is when the Cleveland Browns decided to use the number three draft pick on the 2007 NFL Draft on Joe Thomas. It was genius as Thomas is easily the greatest Cleveland Brown of their new era.

He got off to an amazing start as a Cleveland Brown and never looked back. He was named the NFL's Rookie of the Month for November 2007. He was selected to the 2008 Pro Bowl, replacing Jason Peters of the Buffalo Bills. He was named to the NFL All-Rookie Team and came in second in the voting for NFL Rookie of the Year. He was the only player to receive votes besides the eventual winner, Adrian Peterson.

After four seasons of watching Thomas start and play in every game, along with four straight Pro Bowl appearances, the Browns were smart enough to know what they had in him. Thomas and the Browns agreed to a record-setting seven-year, $84 million extension with $44 million guaranteed before the 2012 season.

Thomas started every single game in the 2007–2016 seasons. He was starting and playing offensive snap through the first seven games of 2017 season as well before getting hurt against Tennessee and requiring season-ending surgery. He decided to retire from the NFL shortly after that. He played and started in 167 consecutive games as a Cleveland Brown, a record for a lineman that will never be touched again. In April 2020, Thomas was named to the NFL 2010s All-Decade team by NFL beat writers as of 6,680 pass blocking attempts, Thomas allowed only thirty sacks during his career.

He is perhaps the greatest offensive lineman to never play in the postseason as the Browns went 48–128 during that stretch. He played 10,363 consecutive snaps while being voted to ten Pro Bowls, six first-team All-Pro selections, and two second-team All-Pro selections during his eleven seasons. He has widely been regarded as one of the greatest offensive linemen in NFL history. He was put on the NFL Hall of Fame ballot in November of 2022.

Joshua Cribbs was a multipurpose threat while playing quarterback at Kent State. As a Golden Flash, he is the all-time total offense leader with 10,839 yards. Other school records include rushing touchdowns (38), pass completions (616), pass attempts (1,123), passing yardage (7,169), touchdowns scored (41), and points scored (246).

He is one of only two true freshman in National Collegiate Athletic Association (NCAA) history to both rush and pass for 1,000 yards (the other being Armanti Edwards of Appalachian State). He is also one of only eight players in NCAA history to both rush and pass for 1,000 yards in at least two different seasons. He is one of only four quarterbacks in NCAA history to rush for 3,500 yards and throw for 7,000 yards in his career.

Despite solid numbers in the MAC, Cribbs was not chosen in the 2005 NFL Draft; however, he was signed as an undrafted free agent by the Cleveland Browns on April 29, 2005, and invited to come to camp for a possible spot on the team as a wide receiver. Despite years of bad quarterback play in Cleveland, he was never given a chance to compete or quarterback and instead, worked his butt off to learn a new position at wideout. He was also designated for special teams, a move that would impact his entire career for the better.

The hard work paid off for Cribbs; after just one season, Cribbs signed a six-year contract extension with the Browns following his rookie season that saw him average 24.5 yards per kick return, and his total of

1,094 return yards set a franchise record. He also took one all the way, which was a sign of things to come as in a game against the Detroit Lions, he returned a kick ninety yards for his first NFL touchdown.

The only thing missing was him as an offensive threat, as he never carried the ball on a Jet Sweep or any kind of run, and only had one pass reception. 2006 wasn't much better in those categories with only ten catches for ninety-one yards.

Where he really began making a serious impact was the kick return game. In 2006 he set a new franchise record for most kickoff yardage in a season, breaking the record he had set the year prior. Cribbs took off for 1,494 returns yards on sixty-one kick returns with a touchdown. He was one of the lone bright spots during a horrendous 2006 season.

In 2007, Cribbs exploded onto the NFL map as the Browns went 10–6 and there were more eyes on the team in general. Cribbs added punt returns into this game with 30 of them for 405 yards and a touchdown. On the kick returning side, he had a career high of 1,809 yards on 59 returns with 2 touchdowns. Cribbs was voted to the 2008 Pro Bowl as a kick returner for the AFC. Cribbs had one kick-return touchdown in each of his first three years in the NFL.

In 2008, Cribbs showed no signs of slowing down and kept the show going as he had a touchdown on a kickoff return, scoring on a 92-yard return versus the Baltimore Ravens in week 9. It was the fifth kickoff return touchdown of Cribbs's career. Cribbs also had a four-yard rushing touchdown against the Buffalo Bills in a Monday Night Football game. On November 26, 2008, after placing Brady Quinn on injured reserve, the Browns named Cribbs their emergency quarterback as he once again showed he could be the ultimate team player if needed. He finished with 1,110 kick return yards on the season along with 228 punt returns yards.

2009 was a bad year for Cleveland Browns football, but one that gave Cribbs a few chances to shine in the darkest of times. Several times in 2009 Cribbs would do something outstanding that gave Browns fans at least a little something to puff their chests out about. He had 3 touchdowns returning kicks, 1 touchdown returning punts, 1 touchdown on the ground, and 4 receiving for a career-high 9 touchdown season. He did it all!

On September 13, in the Browns' home opener versus the Minnesota Vikings, Cribbs returned a punt sixty-seven yards for a touchdown, tying the team record for career returns for a touchdown (seven) with Eric Metcalf. Also, in that same game, Cribbs was named as a starting wide receiver for the first time in his NFL career.

On October 18, Cribbs returned a Pittsburgh kickoff for a touchdown, breaking the team record for returns for a touchdown. In this game he became the first NFL player to throw an interception and record a kickoff return touchdown in the same game since 1950.

On December 10, Cribbs led the Browns to victory over the Pittsburgh Steelers, their first win over their rival in 13 games. Cribbs led all offensive players with 200 all-purpose yards, including 87 yards rushing out of the Wildcat formation.

On December 20, Cribbs returned two kickoffs for touchdowns against the Kansas City Chiefs to set and extend the all-time NFL record for most kickoff returns for touchdowns in a career. On December 29, Cribbs was named to the 2010 Pro Bowl for the second time in his career as the Browns' and AFC's representative as the kick returner. Cribbs was also named the Browns' team MVP for the 2009 season.

Relations between Cribbs and the Browns soured at the end of the 2009 season, as negotiations on a new contract extension ended with a reported $1.4 million per year offer that Cribbs felt was insultingly low considering everything he did to help the team.

Tensions boiled over on January 7, 2010, when Cribbs cleaned out his locker at the Browns' training complex and announced his intention to walk out on the final three years of his contract. The Browns were able to calm the storm and talk him into sticking around as on March 5, 2010, Cribbs re-signed with the Cleveland Browns with a three-year, $20 million contract.

Perhaps the off-the-field money drama caused an issue however, as 2010 was the first season he fell short of 1,000 kick returning with only 814 yards and no touchdowns on either kickoff returns or punt returns.

His biggest play of the season came week 2 at home against Kansas City. The Browns were in a close game with the Chiefs, down 10–7 in the second quarter, when backup quarterback Seneca Wallace connected on a sixty-five-yard touchdown pass to Cribbs to put the Browns ahead 14–13 in the second quarter. Two second half Ryan Succop field goals along with zero points from Cleveland would lead to the 16–14 loss.

2011 was another solid year for Cribbs despite a major rule change in the NFL. The 2011 season marked the year of the NFL's rule change on kickoffs, shifting the position from the kicking team's own 30-yard line to the 35. The move intended to prevent more returns due to the violent collisions that they sometimes yielded. Cribbs saw his return numbers dwindle somewhat from the rule change, and the market value for specialized return men had dwindled as well.

With his role as a kick returner having to take a five-yard step back, he focused even more on other areas of his game and how he could help the team. Cribbs set a career-high of 41 receptions, 518 yards, and 4 touchdowns. He also had an 84-yard punt return for a touchdown.

Cribbs would go on to play one more season (2012) with the Browns, before leaving after the season for other avenues in the NFL. By the time he was done in Cleveland, Cribbs had 110 catches for 1,175 yards and 7 touchdowns. He ran the ball in the Wildcat formation or Jet Sweeps for 797 yards on 140 attempts with 2 touchdowns. 222 punt returns for 2,375 yards and 3 touchdowns.

Now, none of those numbers would sell a single jersey, a single trading card, or even get fans talking about him on social media. It was the 11,113 kickoff return yards along with an NFL record eight return touchdowns that may never be broken with the new rules in place. Most of all, it was his heart that will be cherished by Cleveland Browns fans forever!

While Cribbs, Thomas, and Dawson all have solid arguments for possible placement in the NFL Hall of Fame one day, there are still several Cleveland Browns moments and players that will live in forever lore for their contributions to the franchise's legacy.

On December 20, 2009, at Kansas City, Cleveland Browns running back Jerome Harrison broke Jim Brown's single-game rushing record for a Cleveland Browns running back with 286 yards and 3 touchdowns, placing him third on the all-time single-game rushing yards list behind Adrian Peterson, who had rushed for 296 yards and 3 touchdowns against the San Diego Chargers in 2007, and Jamal Lewis, who had rushed for 295 yards and 2 touchdowns against the Browns in 2003. He maintained that form through the end of the regular season, rushing for 561 yards and 5 touchdowns in the last three games. Harrison signed a 1-year, $2 million contract at the end of 2009 and became the starting running back for the Browns at the start of the 2010 season.

This game by Harrison against the Chiefs was part of a wild stretch for Cleveland as they followed up a hideous 1–11 start to the 2009 season to win their last four games with a 13–6 win over Pittsburgh on a frozen night in Cleveland, a 41–34 win over Kansas City with Harrison's record-setting performance and 2 kickoff return touchdowns by Joshua Cribbs in a wild game that saw 75 points. They would close the year with wins at home over Oakland 23–9 and Jacksonville 23–17.

The crazy thing about 2010, however, was that it was another Cleveland Browns running back who would steal the show, and become one hell of a one-year wonder. Peyton Hillis attended Conway High School in Conway, Arkansas, and was a highly touted recruit. Hillis attended the University of Arkansas where he was primarily used as a fullback.

After being drafted in the seventh round of the 2008 NFL Draft, Hillis rose to the top of the depth chart as the starting fullback for the Denver Broncos. Due to injuries to the running back corps, he became the starting running back. After spending two years in Denver, Hillis was traded to the Cleveland Browns in 2010.

His 2010 season in Cleveland is a thing of wonder as he rushed for 1,177 yards on 270 carries with 11 touchdowns to go along with 61 for 477 yards and 2 touchdowns. Hillis played well with starting quarterbacks Jake Delhomme, Seneca Wallace, and Colt McCoy as he was the one constant all season long that just kept delivering.

In Cleveland's only win over New England during the stretch of 2000–2022, it was Hillis having an amazing game in 2010 to lead the Browns to a 34–14 win over Bill Belichick, Tom Brady, and the New England Patriots. Hillis rushed for a career-high 184 yards on 29 carries with 2 rushing touchdowns. Following this game, Hillis was named AFC

Offensive Player of the Week for week 9, the first Cleveland Browns running back to win that honor since Eric Metcalf in 1992.

His ascent over Harrison as top back started earlier in the year when Hillis was promoted into the starting spot for a week 3 game versus the Baltimore Ravens. The result was a 144-yard (6.5 ypc) romp against the Ravens' staunch rushing defense, which allowed just 3.4 yards per carry in the 2009 season. Hillis also added 36 yards on 7 receptions for a total of 180 all-purpose yards.

The next week, Hillis again ran for over 100 yards at home against the Cincinnati Bengals, leading the Browns to their first victory in the 2010 regular season. In week 5 against the Atlanta Falcons, Hillis had a nineteen-yard reception for a touchdown, making him the first Browns player since Greg Pruitt to record touchdowns in five consecutive games.

In week 12, Hillis joined Marshall Faulk as the only players to have achieved more than 130 yards rushing, 3 rushing touchdowns, and 60 yards receiving in a single game with his massive performance in a 24–23 win at Carolina. His big year led to him winning a nationwide contest to be placed on the cover of the Madden 2012 Video Game by EA Sports.

The 2010 season was an anomaly in many ways, however, as it also featured the debut of the beloved Texas quarterback legend Colt McCoy who many Browns fans thought would be the next Bernie Kosar. The season started off with someone completely different, though, as Cleveland signed former Carolina Panthers Super Bowl–appearing quarterback Jake Delhomme.

On March 13, 2010, Delhomme signed a two-year deal with the Cleveland Browns and easily won the starting quarterback job over Seneca Wallace after competing with him during training camp. However, he suffered a high ankle sprain during the second quarter of the Browns' first game of the season, a loss to the Tampa Bay Buccaneers. Delhomme wouldn't return until week 5 at home against Atlanta.

Prior to the injury, the Browns and their fans had high hopes for Delhomme from everything he overcame and achieved in Carolina. After spending six years in NFL Europe, he finally got his chance to play in the NFL in 2003 with the Panthers. The Panthers had been struggling, and were just one season removed from a dismal 1–15 season, during which they set a then-NFL record for consecutive losses in a single season. Although Rodney Peete was the Panthers' starter, Delhomme was looked at to be the future of the franchise.

At halftime of the 2003 season opener against the Jacksonville Jaguars, the Panthers were down 14–0. Delhomme took over for Peete and threw three touchdowns, the last coming in a fourth-down situation with just sixteen seconds left in the game, to lead the Panthers to a comeback victory. Panther head coach John Fox wanted to keep with the hot hand; thus he started the following week against the Tampa Bay Buccaneers, and proceeded to start every game during the 2003 season.

The move to Delhomme was the perfect answer as, including the playoffs, Delhomme led the Panthers on eight game-winning drives in the fourth quarter or overtime in the 2003 season, the most game-winning drives any QB has ever had in a single season. The "Jake Magic" was felt in the playoffs as well as he led them to a Super Bowl appearance after a double-overtime victory against the St. Louis Rams and then defeating the first-seeded Philadelphia Eagles in the NFC Championship game, the Panthers made it through to Super Bowl XXXVIII to face the New England Patriots.

He lit it up in the Super Bowl with a masterful 16-of-33 for 323 yards, 3 passing touchdowns, no interceptions, and a 113.6 passer rating performance. He also set a record for longest offensive play from scrimmage in Super Bowl history with an 85-yard pass to Muhsin Muhammad. If it wasn't for a last-minute field goal by Adam Vinatieri, the Panthers would have won and Delhomme would have been the MVP.

His next six seasons in Carolina were up and down, but with no return trips to the big game. He would finish his time in Carolina with 19,258 yards passing and 120 touchdowns. He also led the Panthers to the NFC's best record in 2008 with a 12–4 mark. The Browns were getting someone they could trust behind center and finally ending the ongoing Brady Quinn versus Derek Anderson drama at the same time by cutting both.

Delhomme's return from injury week 5 against Atlanta as he was noticeably not 100 percent while playing and ultimately reinjured his ankle in a dismal 20–10 loss to the Falcons. Enter the next great hope of Cleveland football, Colt McCoy.

The run of Colt McCoy in Cleveland was very short, but my goodness, was it fun—for a brief fleeting moment, it seemed as though he would be the next big thing in Cleveland sports. In 2006, after spending his redshirted freshman season behind Vince Young as The University of Texas won the National Championship, Colt would finally get his chance to lead the Longhorns. After winning out a close competition with Jevan Snead, McCoy became the 2006 starting quarterback for the University of Texas. The season opener saw McCoy lead the Longhorns to a 56–7 victory over North Texas, throwing for three touchdowns and rushing a yard for another, while throwing no interceptions.

He was 12–19 in passing, and ran for 27 yards to help set up a touchdown. In only his second pass as a college quarterback McCoy threw a 60-yard touchdown pass. He was the first Texas freshman quarterback to start and win a season-opening game since Bobby Layne in 1944. Following wins over Rice, Iowa State, and Sam Houston State, McCoy got his first win over a ranked team, as well as his first come-from-behind victory, when he led the Longhorns over rival Oklahoma 28–10 in the Red River Shootout. McCoy threw for two touchdowns in the game.

The two touchdowns by McCoy gave him twelve touchdown passes for the season, tied for third with Longhorn passer James Brown in the list of most touchdowns by a Texas freshman. He was just getting started. On October 14, 2006, McCoy threw a Texas record six touchdown passes in the win against Baylor. In the 2006 Oklahoma State game McCoy threw for his twenty-seventh passing touchdown of the season, giving him sole possession of the single-season Texas record and putting him two touchdowns shy of the NCAA single season record for freshman quarterbacks (29).

He just kept pouring it on during his sophomore year in 2007 with Texas as in the road opener was the first game ever played in the new home stadium of the UCF Knights. McCoy's 47 passing attempts tied a Texas single-game record. His 32 completions set a new school record, besting the 30 completed by Vince Young during the 2006 Rose Bowl and by Major Applewhite during two 1999 games.

It was just the beginning of a great season for Colt McCoy as by the time they reached bowl season he had 21 touchdowns and over 3,000 yards. In the 2007 Holiday Bowl, against Arizona State, McCoy led the Longhorns to a 52–34 victory and won the offensive-player MVP award.

As the 2008 season began and the nation's attention was on Florida quarterback Tim Tebow, it was McCoy who just kept pouring it on. He didn't need the constant national attention and just continued to shine as on January 5, 2009, McCoy led the Longhorns to a 24–21 victory over Ohio State in the Fiesta Bowl. McCoy completed 41-of-59 passes for 414 yards, 2 touchdowns, and 1 interception. He was named the Offensive Player of the Game for his performance.

This was the perfect conclusion to a huge season that saw McCoy named the 2008 AP Big 12 Offensive Player of the Year. Heading into the bowl game he had already had 3,594 passing yards for the season with 2 touchdowns.

Heading into 2010, with the National spotlight continuing to shine solely on guys like Florida quarterback Tim Tebow and Oklahoma quarterback Sam Bradford, McCoy just kept balling out. He led the Texas Longhorns to a perfect 12–0 regular season record, as well as a 13–12 victory over the Nebraska Cornhuskers to win the Big 12 Championship. He became the most victorious quarterback in NCAA history with 45 career wins. Under the direction of McCoy, the Longhorn offense scored 550 points in 2009.

McCoy led the Longhorns to the 2009 National Championship game where the Longhorns took on the heavily favored Alabama Crimson Tide. Sadly, he left the 2010 BCS National Championship Game during Texas' first offensive drive early in the first quarter with a right shoulder injury and was sidelined for the remainder of the game. McCoy was replaced by true freshman quarterback Garrett Gilbert. Alabama would go on to win the game 37–21. Despite the sad ending, his UT career was a giant success as he finished with a career record of 45–8 including 112 touchdowns passes and 13,253 yards.

McCoy was a folk hero in Texas and was now coming to a quarterback-starved town who desperately wanted him to work out so they could love him. McCoy was drafted in the third round as the eighty-fifth overall pick by the Cleveland Browns in the 2010 NFL Draft. Pointing out that Cleveland already had three quarterbacks, Browns president Mike Holmgren said McCoy would likely not play his first season with the team in order to develop him as an NFL quarterback. However, that plan was nuked by week 6 when starting quarterback Jake Delhomme and backup Seneca Wallace were both sidelined and McCoy made his first career start against the Pittsburgh Steelers.

It wasn't the ideal first start, but it wasn't bad either as McCoy completed 23 of 33 passes for 281 yards, a touchdown, and 2 interceptions in the Browns' loss. He also scrambled 4 times for 22 yards. It was what he did the next two weeks that had fans buzzing when the following week against the New Orleans Saints he led the Browns to a shocking victory over the defending Super Bowl champions 30–17 at the Louisiana Superdome in New Orleans.

If that wasn't enough to get everyone excited, the following week, thanks to the big day from Hillis mentioned earlier, on November 7, McCoy made his third consecutive start and led the Browns to another upset victory, this time against the New England Patriots 34–14.

The Browns were suddenly 3–5 and back in contention as McCoy had Cleveland feeling really good! The following week he led the Browns on a last-second, two-minute drive to tie the game against the AFC powerhouse New York Jets and force overtime. The Browns would ultimately lose the game 26–20, but McCoy continued to show he could handle the big moments.

McCoy finished his rookie season starting eight games, with a 2–6 record, and with six touchdowns against nine interceptions but none of that mattered because all fans wanted to talk about and remember was those back-to-back stunning wins over New England and New Orleans led by McCoy.

In 2011 McCoy became the full-time starter for the Browns. In the home opener against the Cincinnati Bengals, McCoy completed 19 of 40 attempts for 213 yards with two touchdowns and one interception in a 27–17 loss. The next two weeks, the Browns defeated the Indianapolis Colts and the Miami Dolphins with McCoy throwing combined 41 of 71 attempts, 421 yards, and three touchdowns with one interception in back-to-back come from behind wins over Indy and Miami. The win over the Dolphins coming with a last second touchdown drive!

Injuries and bad decisions by personnel running the team derailed his time in Cleveland, but those brief moments will forever live in Browns fans hearts! Everyone just wanted to love and be like Colt McCoy!

Don't believe me? Colt was so popular with teammates and fans in college that country musician Aaron Watson wrote and performed a song about Colt at his wedding in July of 2010 to Rachel Glandorf. The song was titled, "When I Grow Up I Want to Be Just Like Colt McCoy."

CHAPTER 8

# Defeating the Enemy

THE PITTSBURGH STEELERS VERSUS THE CLEVELAND BROWNS IS PER-
haps the greatest rivalry in the history of the National Football League.
Fans will talk about the Bears versus the Packers, the Cowboys versus the
Redskins, and even the Raiders versus the Broncos, but for my money,
nothing says drama like when these two teams hook it up.

What really drives this rivalry is the proximity of the two cities being
less than 150 miles apart and both having fan bases that travel well. There
are nearly 400 Browns Backers groups plastered all over the world.

If you count the AAFL and the NFL, the Browns have won 8 total
championships. They won 4 in the AAFL in 1946, 1947, 1948, and 1949.
Then, when they entered the NFL and not many around the league gave
them a chance, they instantly started dominating there by winning championships in 1950, 1954, 1955, and 1964. That is more world championships than any other team in the history of professional football.

The Steelers are not far behind with six NFL Superbowl Championships of their own. The Steelers won those rings at Super Bowls IX, XI,
XIII, XIV, XL, and XLIII. They defeated the Dallas Cowboys twice, and
the Rams, Minnesota Vikings, Seattle Seahawks, and Arizona Cardinals
once each. Four of the Six Super Bowl championships came in the 1970s
with players such as Franco Harris, Terry Bradshaw, Lynn Swann, and
John Stallworth, just to name a few.

Both teams are steeped in legacy with an abundance of Hall of
Famers as each is known as a football town. It doesn't matter how many
NHL titles the Pittsburgh Penguins brought to town in the 1990s, or the

Pirates World Series Championships in the 1970s. Pittsburgh is black and gold for the Steelers first and foremost.

I mentioned Hall of Famers—the two franchises have a combined total of 46 players enshrined in Canton. Totals include 29 from Pittsburgh and 17 from Cleveland. Had the Browns not left the league for 3 years and stumbled through mediocrity since their return, there would be a lot more combined.

The Cleveland Browns Hall of Famers include Paul Brown, Joe DeLamielleure, Len Ford, Frank Gatski, Otto Graham, Lou Groza, Gene Hickerson, Leroy Kelly, Dante Lavelli, Mike McCormack, Bobby Mitchell, Marion Motley, Ozzie Newsome, Paul Warfield, Bill Willis, and Mac Speedie.

The two franchises have clashed 142 times following their week 3 matchup in the 2022 regular season. At that time, Pittsburgh led the all-time series 79–62–1. The Browns led the series before leaving the league in 1995, but have struggled upon return.

The teams began hooking it up in 1950 on October 7, 1950, when the Browns captured a 30–17 victory. This began a nice streak of wins for Cleveland to show early dominance in the feud as they won the first 8 meetings between the teams, and the Browns would go on to win the first 16 of 18 matchups between the teams headed in to the 1959 season. This was well before the Steelers began to become a premier force in the NFL, and the Browns were routinely one of the best teams, if not the best team in the entire league.

The Browns' dominance of the rivalry would extend through the 1960s as well; it got to the point that after they battled twice in 1969, the all-time record stood 30–8 in massive favor of the Browns. The 1970s clearly began to sway things in favor of the black and gold, however, as that is when the Super Bowl years began in Pittsburgh. During the 10-year period in the 1970s as the two teams began to trade places, the Steelers won 15 of 20 matchups between the two squads. At one point, the Steelers rattled off 6 straight wins as they swept the seasons series in 1977, 1978, and 1979.

By the time 1980 rolled around it was a true rivalry as both teams were much closer in the win column and the games were starting to become more dramatic and passion-filled every time. Two of the losses to Pittsburgh in the late 1970s were in overtime, and that just ramped things up.

It wasn't until about the mid-1980s when things turned back in favor of the Browns as they began a run of 7 straight wins over Pittsburgh starting with the back to back thrilling wins in 1986. That is where I will choose to start listing some of my personal favorite Browns victories in the rivalry, beginning in 1986 when I was old enough to start watching and paying close attention.

## 1986 SEASON, WEEK 5 AT PITTSBURGH
*Cleveland 27, Pittsburgh 24*
The Browns built a 10–0 lead after one quarter on the strength of a touchdown pass from Bernie Kosar to Webster Slaughter and a 15-yard field off the foot of Matt Bahr. The Steelers would bounce back by scoring the next 14 points, all in the second quarter to take a 14–10 lead with only 58 seconds left in the first half before Gerald "Ice Cube" McNeil took a kickoff 100 yards to the house to give the Browns a 17–14 lead.

The Steelers would wrap a Louis Lipps touchdown catch and Gary Anderson field goal around a Matt Bahr field goal to increase their lead to 24–20 with the game winding down. It was then that Kosar gave Browns fans a glimpse at the exciting days ahead with a thrilling road comeback. Kosar led a quick strike drive as the clock wound down which led to Earnest Byner scoring from four yards out to put Cleveland ahead 27–24 to stay.

## 1986 SEASON, WEEK 12 IN CLEVELAND
*Cleveland 37, Pittsburgh 31 in overtime*
*"The Monday Night Thriller"*
This game was a major turning point in the season as the Browns held a 7–4 record coming in, and they proceeded to win their final five games with this game being the spark. The overtime wins against their divisional rival further showed the dominance at home and rising prominence the Browns had in the division.

Bernie Kosar played great all season as the permanent leader of the team. Kosar started all 16 games, completing 310 passes for 3,854 yards and 17 touchdowns but this was easily his shining game and his coming-out party as the face of the franchise. Kosar went off that night for 414 yards on 289 of 46 passing with 2 touchdowns. The crowning shot came in overtime with all the chips on the table as he eluded heavy pressure to launch a 36-yard touchdown pass to his number one threat Webster Slaughter.

## 1987 SEASON WEEK 2 IN CLEVELAND
*Cleveland 34, Pittsburgh 10*
*"Pick City"*

Following a scoreless first quarter by both teams, it was all Browns as they dominated the Steelers for the remaining three quarters. The Steelers cut into the lead to 17–10 at one point, before the Browns finished the game with 17 straight points to finish the 34–10 route in a laugher. Bernie threw for 2 touchdowns and 174 yards while Kevin Mack and Earnest Byner ran for 53 yards each in the win. It was the Browns defense that stole the show however as they picked off Pittsburgh quarterbacks Mark Malone and Bubby Brister a combined 6 times.

## 1987 SEASON WEEK 16
*Cleveland 19, Pittsburgh 13 in Pittsburgh*
*"Christmas Comes Late for Browns Fans"*

Headed into the final game of the 1987 season, the Browns needed a win. They were 9–4 in a strike altered season and needed a win to get a bye in the first round of the playoffs. The 8–6 Steelers stood in their way and this being the day after Christmas, a short travel day wouldn't make things any easier on Cleveland. The Browns have had a history of closing the season in Pittsburgh, and this was just one of many times to come.

The game itself didn't have a ton of flash to it, as the Browns ground out a victory. Kosar threw for 241 yards and a touchdown while getting sacked twice and picked off once. Mack and Byner once again combined to rush for over 100 yards as the Browns played tough defense and never let Pittsburgh put much together in the season-ending win.

## 1988 Season Week 5 at Pittsburgh
*Cleveland 23, Pittsburgh 9*
"Pagel Steps Up"

A quarter of the way into the season, the Browns had used three starting quarterbacks and were desperate for answers to get the train back on the tracks. They traveled to Pittsburgh with Mike Pagel at the helm. However, quarterback play would have little to do with the Browns 23–9 victory that Sunday. Matt Bahr kicked 3 field goals combined with a 75 yard interception for a touchdown by Brian Washington that was more than enough for the win. They coupled the solid defense with a strong running game as Earnest Byner had 78 yards on 20 carries. Tim Manoa was also a bright spot chipping in with 82 yards on 18 carries including a touchdown.

## 1988 Season Week 12 in Cleveland
*Cleveland 27, Pittsburgh 7*
"Bernie Returns to Beat Their Rivals"

The Browns were determined to turn things around once again after two straight brutal conference losses. Their archrival the Pittsburgh Steelers were coming to town and the Browns wasted no time taking out their frustration against their hated rivals. The Browns built an early big lead and never looked back. Bernie Kosar threw touchdown passes to Reggie Langhorne and Derek Tennell. Frank Minnifield chipped in with an excellent special team's effort as he returned a blocked punt for a touchdown. The Steelers were no match for the inspired Browns attack, and Cleveland won 27–7, improving their record to 7–5 three-quarters of the way into the season.

## 1989 Season, Week 1
*Cleveland 51, Pittsburgh 0*
"Bud's First Game"

When Coach Schottenheimer left Cleveland after the 1988 season, he would be leaving behind some very big shoes to fill, the question was, who would fill them? Schottenheimer had led the resurgence of the

Browns after bringing them to the playoffs four straight season. Would they turn to someone already on the staff, or look outside the franchise for someone with prior head coaching experience? Marty had been the full-time head coach for four seasons, leading them to the playoffs each season. It was a strange move for Modell to make, but it was made even stranger when he looked to someone who made his name while working for the enemy to become the new head coach.

Without Marty at the helm, the Browns would need to succeed him with someone who could handle the talent on the team but also the ego of the owner. The fact that the team had been to the playoffs four years in a row and had one of the league's best offensive attacks would help make it a lucrative employment opportunity for any established coach looking to get back into the league, or any top-notch assistant looking to make a name for himself.

The solution for head coach came from the most unusual of places as it was a man who made his name as being one of the most important assistant coaches of the Browns' hated divisional rivals, the Pittsburgh Steelers. The new head coach of the Browns would now be Leon Carson, or as everyone knew him, Bud.

The Bud Carson era of the Browns would begin on September 10, 1989, from the steel city of Pittsburgh. Carson was in the same city in which he had seen his best success in the NFL as the defensive coordinator of the vaunted steel curtain. It was at Three Rivers Stadium in front of a packed house of Steelers fans.

The Steelers were led that year by quarterback Bubby Brister, who the games television announcer Joe Namath was quoted on the broadcast as saying, "Brister all set to make things happen today." Brister's main receiving threats were rookie receiver Derek Hill and Louis Lipps. In the backfield with Brister was rookie running back Tim Worley and veteran fullback and resident loudmouth Meril Hoge. However, despite the boast of Namath in the booth, the only thing that Brister was able to "make happen" was turnovers and bad plays as the Browns crushed the Steelers from the opening snap!

The Browns came out like a house on fire to impress their new head coach and help him take home a victory against his ex-team, and their hated rivals. The defensive scheme of Carson paid immediate dividends when linebacker Clay Mathews took a fumble in for a touchdown and gave the Browns the early 7–0 lead. After a Matt Bahr field goal made it 10–0, the defense scored again when this time it was linebacker David Grayson taking another fumble in for a touchdown. At the end of the first quarter, it was Cleveland 17, Pittsburgh 0, with both touchdowns being scored by the Browns' hungry defense. Despite the boast of Namath of the unproven Brister, it was the Browns' defense that was truly making things happen that day.

The scoring spree for the Browns continued in the second quarter when Matt Bahr booted another field goal, this from twenty yards and put the Browns up 20–0. They captured their first offensive score when Tim Manoa rumbled in the end zone from three yards out later in the quarter. Matt Bahr capped off the first half scoring with a successful thirty-yard field goal to send the Browns into the locker room at halftime up 30–0.

The Browns continued to pour on the scoring in the second half as they opened up the third quarter with another Tim Manoa touchdown rumble. This one from two yards out and put the Browns even further ahead by a score of 37–0. The defense wasn't done scoring yet either, as moments later it was David Grayson scoring his second touchdown of the game; this time it was a fourteen-yard interception return. At the end of three quarters, it was the Browns dominating the Steelers 44–0. The Browns would tack on one more touchdown with a Mike Oliphant twenty-one-yard touchdown rushing strike.

When the bloodbath was done, it was the Cleveland Browns 51 and the Pittsburgh Steelers 0. It was one of the biggest opening day blowouts in NFL history. Kosar didn't have to do too much as he had short fields to work on all day because of the incredible defensive play. He threw for 207 yards, including a 51-yard strike to Webster Slaughter to set up one of the touchdowns.

The newly minted three-headed rushing attack did not do anything to overly impress, but they did get the job done when needed. The rookie Eric Metcalf had a modest 28 yards on 10 carries. Mike Oliphant who was only seeing increased playing time because of the Kevin Mack imprisonment, ran for 48 yards on 6 carries, including the 21-yard touchdown strike. Tim Manoa rushed the ball 9 times for only 20 yards, but did score twice from within the 5-yard line. Matt Bahr would have to ice down his foot on the plane ride home as he kicked six extra points and three field goals for a total of 13 points.

As for Bubby Brister, the man who Namath claimed would "really make things happen" went a meager 10 for 22 passing with only 84 yards. Brister compounded those weak numbers with three interceptions and six sacks. The Browns defense had dominated in the opening week, and put the rest of the AFC on notice! It was also the worst home loss of legendary Pittsburgh head coach Chuck Noll's long coaching career.

## 1990 SEASON, WEEK 1 IN CLEVELAND
*Cleveland 13, Pittsburgh 3*
*"Getting Off on the Right Foot"*

Perhaps it was a hangover from their third AFC Championship game loss in four years, or maybe they just weren't ready to go yet, but week 1 appeared to be a clunker as the Browns trailed the Steelers 3–0 after a lackluster first half. As the game progressed, the Browns wouldn't score a single point by their offense, and rather had to settle for two Jerry Kauric field goals and a defensive fumble return touchdown by Anthony Blaylock for the ho-hum 13–3 lead. It wasn't pretty, but little did anyone know that "boring" win would be one of only three opening week wins they would secure over the next thirty-plus years!

## 1991 SEASON, WEEK 8 IN CLEVELAND
*Cleveland 17, Pittsburgh 14*
*"Bill Wins His Pittsburgh Debut"*

It was another low-scoring affair, but a Leroy Hoard touchdown catch combined with a one-yard touchdown run from Kevin Mack was enough to give them the 17–14 victory. Kosar remained consistent as he threw for 179 yards and a touchdown with zero interceptions. The Browns had bounced back from the three-game losing streak to win two straight and climb back to .500 at 4–4 at the middle point of the season.

Things weren't looking too bad for Belichick as his first eight games of an NFL coach went better than he could have hoped for. To be .500 this far into your first season was an accomplishment in itself. Things would get a lot harder for the rookie head coach and the Browns, however, as they would finish 2–6 in their final eight games, to end the season at 6–10.

## 1992 Season, Week 5 in Cleveland
### *Cleveland 17, Pittsburgh 9*
*"Mike Tomczak Proves to Be Adequate"*

With the suddenly injury-prone Bernie Kosar continuing to age and playing behind a shaky offense line, the Browns knew they would need a suitable replacement in 1992 ready to come in for Bernie when he got hurt. The Browns brain trust, namely Belichick wasn't sold on Kosar to begin with, and was always looking for a possible replacement if need be. That year's search led them to acquiring former Chicago Bears starting quarterback Mike Tomczak.

Mike Tomczak was no stranger to replacing a beloved veteran as he did in Chicago when he took over for Jim McMahon, a Super Bowl–winning quarterback and crowd favorite. Fans from Cleveland already knew of him from his time as the starting quarterback for the Ohio State Buckeyes.

He had won Illinois High School Player of the Year honors while playing at Thornton Fractional North High School in Calumet City where he was coached by his father Ron Tomczak. This led to him being awarded an athletic scholarship to Ohio State. He proved to be a winner at Ohio State and led the Buckeyes to a couple of Big Ten Championships.

Despite his success in both high school and college, Tomczak went undrafted out of college and signed as an original free agent with the Chicago Bears. While playing with the Bears his rookie season, he didn't see much playing time but was lucky enough to be a part of the Super Bowl–winning team. When he eventually took over for McMahon things went well as he won his first ten starts at quarterback, which set an NFL record.

While starting in Chicago, he proved to be the man for the job as he led them back to the playoffs in 1988. He also showed he could play in bad weather as he was the starting QB for Chicago in the infamous "Fog Bowl" playoff game against the Philadelphia Eagles. The Bears won the game, earning them a trip to the NFC Championship Game.

Mike Tomczak would eventually fall out of favor in Chicago and sign with the Green Bay Packers. This was before the epic starting streak of Brett Favre began, which actually allowed him a chance to play while in Green Bay. He started in seven games, totaling 11 touchdown passes of his 128 completions and 9 interceptions.

Some in the Green Bay media and other media members around the NFL pegged him to be the next starting quarterback going forward in Green Bay, and as luck would have it he began a lengthy contract hold-out. The Packers didn't feel like playing contract games with Tomczak, and chose to cut him loose instead.

It was a move that would pay off for Green Bay as they opted instead to trade with the Atlanta Falcons for a young man by the name of Brett Favre and let him battle it out with Don Majowksi for the starting role. Favre became the Packers' starting quarterback in the fourth game of the 1992 season, stepping in for injured quarterback Don Majkowski, and started every game through the 2007 season. One can only wonder what would have happened if Tomczak didn't hold out for more money, and whether the legend of Brett Favre may have ever happened.

As the Packers chose to go with the future Hall of Fame quarterback instead of paying Mike Tomczak, the Browns decided that Mike was the man for the job. In the strong chance of Kosar with his diminishing skills going down to injury, they knew Tomczak would be ready if called upon. Keep in mind why this is so notable: the Browns could have traded for Brett Favre and chose not to.

At 1–3, the Browns were back in desperation mode and needed to do anything possible to keep the season afloat as their hated rivals the Pittsburgh Steelers invaded Cleveland Municipal Stadium for week 6 of the NFL season. The Browns made the move to Mike Tomczak for the banged-up Kosar and needed the Steelers game to get back on track.

Not discounting the Steelers, but the Browns were heading toward a lighter spot in their schedule and needed to take advantage of some winnable matchups. They did just that in their contest against the Steelers. Mike Tomczak was steady all day and completed 10 of 17 passes for 171 yards and a touchdown. That touchdown came in the fourth quarter on a 47-yard beautiful strike to Michael Jackson to help put the game away 17–9.

The Browns defense stepped it up big and didn't allow the Steelers offense to cross the goal line all game, instead holding them to three Gary Anderson field goals. Speaking of field goals, it was Matt Stover once again coming through when called upon and hitting a clutch 51-yard field goal of his own earlier in the game. The Jackson touchdown and Stover field goal were complemented by a one-yard Kevin Mack touchdown rumble.

The Kevin Mack touchdown came as a surprise as they hadn't been using him. He emerged from the bench and ran the ball 12 times for 32 yards and the touchdown. Tommy Vardell was limited to three carries for seven yards. Leroy Hoard never saw the field, but Eric Metcalf did get seven attempts for 49 yards. Metcalf also caught three balls for 48 yards.

Most importantly perhaps was the Browns defense holding All-Pro running back Barry Foster to 84 yards on 24 carries, an average less than 4 yards per carry. They also kept Foster out of the end zone which was just as impressive due to his skills. It was a win the Browns sorely needed and were grateful to have.

## 1993 SEASON WEEK 7 IN CLEVELAND
### *Cleveland 28, Pittsburgh 23*
*"The Metcalf Punt Return Game"*

The Browns first round draft pick in 1989 was the speedy Eric Metcalf, a small but fiercely quick running back and kick returner out of Texas University. Metcalf is the son of former St. Louis Cardinal great Terry Metcalf. Not only did Eric have football in his blood, but he had lightning in his feet. He was the 1988 US Track and Field Champion in the long jump and a two-time NCAA Champion in the event while at Texas. It was a talent he developed while in high school as he set records including the seventh longest distance ever posted indoors by a US high schooler with a jump of 7.75 meters.

He continued to excel at track in college as he holds the University of Texas long jump record at 8.44 meters. He went to win the NCAA National Long Jump Championship in 1986 and 1988 and the SWC Long Jump titles in 1986 and 1987. He added on to those accomplishments by also becoming the United States Jr. National Long Jump Champion in 1986 and 1987. His hard work earned him the distinction of being a five-time All-American.

There is no professional track and field, but there is professional football, however, and that is where Metcalf looked to earn a living for himself and also follow in the footsteps of his father. Eric Metcalf excelled in his time at Texas as he was an All-Southwest Conference selection three times. He also was the 1987 Southwest Conference player of the year and a second team All-American. To this day he holds the distinction of being the only player in Texas history to lead the team in all-purpose yards all four years and holds every school receiving record for a running back.

Bernie Kosar coveted pass-catching running backs who could run wild in his pass-happy offense, and the Browns knew that when they drafted Eric Metcalf with their first-round pick, and thirteenth overall pick. The thing about it was since entering the league in 1989, Metcalf constantly had to share the backfield with several other feature backs in Cleveland such as Kevin Mack, Tommy Vardell, and Leroy Hoard. He was never truly given the free pass to be "the guy." Heading into the 1993 season with the Browns, Metcalf had never run for more than 600 yards in a season, and had only done that once. Where he was making his most damage was the kick returning and punt returning game—he was becoming a major threat as he took back several scores in 1992 and was about to do it again in 1993.

The Cleveland Browns had major turmoil going on at quarterback as their hated rivals the Pittsburgh Steelers came to Municipal Stadium. Bernie Kosar has been benched the week before for Vinny Testaverde who was now starting and winning games in replacement of the legend. Vinny Testaverde started the scoring with a sixty-two-yard touchdown pass to Michael Jackson. Eric Metcalf later followed with a ninety-one-yard punt return for a touchdown and the Browns were up 14–0 midway through the second quarter. Pittsburgh responded with their all-pro tailback Barry Foster who scored on two rushing touchdowns to tie the game heading into halftime.

Vinny Testaverde continued to excel and threw for another touchdown pass to Ron Wolfley to put the Browns back in the lead. Three Gary Anderson field goals gave the Steelers back the lead heading into the final minutes of the game. It was then that Testaverde got knocked out of the game with injury. He was 9 for 14 for 167 yards at that point with the two touchdowns and zero interceptions.

With the Browns down 23–21 to their bitter rivals and the beloved Bernie Kosar about to come off the bench and into the game, it almost seemed like a Hollywood scriptoo good to be true. Eric Metcalf removed all the suspense and drama however as he returned the next Pittsburgh punt for a seventy-five-yard touchdown to put the Browns back in the lead.

The Steelers only punted to Eric Metcalf twice, but both times he burned them for a score, totaling 166 yards in the process. Everyone was ready for another epic Kosar comeback, but Metcalf took matters into his own hands giving the Browns the 28–23 victory. It moved the Browns to a division best 5–2 record and once again everything seemed to be right in Browns town. Everything would change eight days later. It was also the last win the original Cleveland Browns ever earned over Pittsburgh.

## 1999 SEASON WEEK 10 IN PITTSBURGH
### *Cleveland 16, Pittsburgh 15*
*"The First Win of the New Rivalry"*

The Browns couldn't have been off to a worse start if they tried, only 1–8 after nine weeks into their new era. With the sole exception of a miracle Hail Mary win at New Orleans, little to nothing had gone right for them and it all started week 1 with an incredibly embarrassing 43–0 loss to Pittsburgh at home in front of 80,000-plus heartbroken fans.

At 1–8, the Browns had nothing to play for but pride as they headed to Pittsburgh that cold afternoon in November. What little motivation they had was the possibility of somehow disturbing Pittsburgh's run toward a playoff bid. Heading into this week, the Steelers were 5–3 heading into this game and right in the thick of things. This loss derailed them so badly, they lost 6 straight, 7 of their last 8, and finished 6–10 in one of the worst finishes in years.

The winning 39-yard field goal by Phil Dawson with no time remaining was a sign of things to come as the placekicker would become the most reliable Cleveland Brown for nearly two decades to follow. The Browns only had 14 first downs all day, and less than 300 total yards, but Dawson showed when given the chance, he could be counted on!

## 2000 SEASON WEEK 3 IN CLEVELAND
### *Cleveland 23, Pittsburgh 20*
*"The Silent Storm Creates Thunder"*

We spoke a lot in the chapter "Rebirth" about Courtney Brown and the hype around him when the Browns drafted him with the first overall pick in the 2000 NFL Draft out of Penn State. While no one can deny his career was a gigantic bust, he played his greatest game just three weeks into his professional career on this day as the Browns stifled their rivals to improve to 2–1 on the season. After a 2–14 season in 1999, the Browns had just tied their season total of wins, only three weeks in!

The biggest reason for this shocking win, the second straight over Pittsburgh since returning, was the play of rookie Courtney Brown. He sacked Pittsburgh quarterback Kent Graham three times in the victory and disrupted anything the Steelers tried all game. The win also moved Tim Couch to 2–0 as a starter against Pittsburgh as he made 316 yards and 2 touchdowns.

The play that stands out the most in my memory of this game is the final drive when Pittsburgh was racing down the field to try and tie the game with a field goal as the clock ticked away. Phil Dawson had put the Browns up 23–20 with a 19-yard field goal, but the Steelers still had 2:48 and a timeout to play with. They dinked and dunked their way down the field with short passes to Mark Bruener, Hines Ward, Bobby Shaw, and Chris Fuamatu-Ma'afala but couldn't get the big hitter to their star Plaxico Burress to stretch the field.

All of this allowed the clock to dribble out quickly, which proved to be a giant and rare mistake from Pittsburgh head coach Bill Cowher. With fourteen seconds left, the Steerers were on the Browns' eight-yard line but were out of timeouts. All they needed to do was avoid a sack, or any place that kept the ball in bounds, and they would get a chance at the game-tying kick to send the game into overtime at the very least. Courtney Brown wrecked all of that for the Steelers as he sacked Kent Graham on third down. It was his shining moment as a Cleveland Brown.

As Pittsburgh tried to hurry their kicking team onto the field, the inexperienced Browns jumped around and celebrated while Brown lined up and got in an all-fours stance, ready to block the possible field goal. Luckily the clock would run out before the Steelers could get the field goal off, but that image of Brown lining up ready to play another down while everyone else celebrated will never leave me.

## 2003 SEASON WEEK 5 AT PITTSBURGH
*Cleveland 33, Pittsburgh 13*
A full review of this game can be found in the chapter, "Prime Time Browns." I will summarize it like this, however. It was clear early on that the Browns had their backs up against the wall to start the 2003 season 1–3 and fading fast. Couch gave them a glimpse at what they thought they were getting when they drafted him as the win pushed them to 2–3 and he looked brilliant throwing for two touchdowns and running for one more.

When they beat the defending AFC Champion Oakland Raiders the next week 13–7, it really gave fans hope that a return to the playoffs was more than possible. Sadly, they would finish the season 5–11, but for one night in Pittsburgh, all felt right with the world. The Browns have not won another regular season game in Pittsburgh since.

## 2009 SEASON WEEK 13 IN CLEVELAND
*Cleveland 13, Pittsburgh 6*
A full review of this game can be found in the chapter, "Prime Time Browns." I will summarize it like this, however. It was well below zero degrees out with the wind chill, and the Browns had won one game in 12

tries coming in. The average amount of defeat the Browns suffered was 16 points a game, by far the worst margin in the NFL. Shockingly they won, defeating the defending Super Bowl Champions and also defeating Big Ben Roethlisberger for the first time ever. He was 9–0 coming into the game. The win led to a four-game win streak to end the season at 11–5, and provide everyone hope once again.

## 2012 SEASON, WEEK 11
### *Cleveland 20, Pittsburgh 14*
The first season with rookie quarterback Brandon Weeden and running back rookie sensation Trent Richardson was off to a miserable start at 2–8. Any chance at a winning season was already well out the window but they still had pride to play for with their rivals coming to town. Heading into this week, the Browns had blown sizable leads against the New York Giants and Dallas Cowboys in recent weeks, and just struggled to maintain confidence. One of their two wins came by the way of a 7–6 slugfest over San Diego, as it was just a strange season.

In fact, things were so odd in 2012, that despite a 2–8 start, if things fell right, they could still make a playoff push if they won their final six games; an 8–8 record may get them in. The AFC was big time down that year, and so was the North. It would have taken a near miracle, but at that moment, hope was still alive and they used that hope to defeat Pittsburgh in front of their hometown fans.

The win came despite Weeden falling prey to his normal faults of holding onto the ball too long and taking 4 sacks to go with an interception. Bailing the Browns out that day was Richardson running for 85 yards on 29 carries with a touchdown. He also caught 4 balls for 27 yards. The defense didn't have to contend with Ben Roethlisberger who was out that day, and shut down former Detroit Lions starting quarterback Charlie Batch. The Browns defense held Batch to 199 yards as they picked him off three times.

As crazy as it seemed, just like it did in 2009, this win sparked a nice winning streak. They used the momentum to win three straight games. The wins came over former Browns starting quarterback Brady Quinn along with head coach Romeo Crennel by the way of a 30–7 victory over the Kansas City Chiefs. They also mixed in a win on the road over the Oakland Raiders thanks in part to a huge night from Josh Gordon who went off for 116 yards, 6 catches, and a touchdown.

At 5–8, they were still on the outside looking in, but that glimmer of hope was still there as they welcomed in the Washington Redskins. The Browns built a 14–10 lead in that one over the then backup quarterback Kirk Cousins but couldn't make it stick. Cousins would go on to throw 329 yards and 2 touchdowns as the Browns playoff hopes ended. Despite the winning streak coming to an end, no one could take it from the Browns that the win over Pittsburgh sparked something and gave fans fun football to watch in November and December, which was rare during this stretch in franchise history.

## 2014 SEASON, WEEK 4
### *Cleveland 31, Pittsburgh 10*
We touched on the 2014 season a bit earlier in the "Prime Time" chapter when we spoke about the Brian Hoyer and Johnny Manziel saga. That portion focused on the big win at Cincinnati on Thursday Night Football that placed the Browns firmly in the playoff hunt and first place in the AFC North. This section placed the emphasis on an early season matchup with Pittsburgh that not only offered incredible revenge, but also bright hope.

Week 1 in Pittsburgh, in the house of horrors known as Hines Field, the Steelers built a 27–3 halftime lead that made it seem as though the Browns were about to get blown out yet again by the Steelers. Fans and media alike were shocked that Johnny Manziel didn't start the second half in place of the struggling Hoyer, but rookie head coach Mike Pettine wasn't ready to make such a move in his first game at the helm.

His faith in Hoyer paid off as the Browns stunned the Steelers with 24 straight points in the first 20 minutes of the second half to tie the game at 27 apiece. The scores came from two touchdown runs by Isaiah Crowell, and a touchdown catch from Travis Benjamin. This, combined with a Billy Cundiff field goal, made it seem like the Browns were on the cusp of an opening weekend miracle!

Sadly, despite the giant comeback and 200 yards rushing, the Browns couldn't pull it off as the Steelers hit a last second field goal from Shaun Suisham from forty-one yards out to win the game. Remarkably, the Browns won in the same fashion the following week over New Orleans on a walk-off field goal by Bull Cundiff. Then, they would lose their week 3 home game against Baltimore as Raven placekicker Justin Tucker hit a walk-off field from thirty-two yards out to defeat Cleveland. It was the first time in NFL history where the same team had their first three games decided on walk-off field goals.

Week 4, it appeared as though a walk-off field goal was the last thing possible as a trip to Nashville turned into a nightmare when the Titans built a 28–3 lead with a few minutes left in the first half. Hoyer then went into hero mode again as he did week 1 versus Pittsburgh, and led the Browns on a wild comeback of 26 straight points to win! The 26 points came thanks in part two a couple of touchdown passes to Travis Benjamin after a wild blocked punt by Tank Harder cut the Titan lead to 28–15 with 11:04 to go. The safety didn't seem big at the time, but those two points proved to be the difference maker.

Now, at 2–2, no one knew what to expect from Cleveland as they welcomed Pittsburgh to town on a sunny Sunday afternoon. They would go on to play their most complete game of the season in a 31–10 win. The 31 points was the most they scored in a game the entire 16-week season. Making that even more interesting is the fact that they were shut out in the first quarter. They would explode for 21 points in the second, and then send the Steelers home as losers in the second half.

It was only their second win over Ben Roethlisberger as they held him in check, Big Ben only threw for 1 touchdown, 228 yards, and was picked off! To the contrary, Hoyer wasn't asked to do too much as he only threw the ball 17 times all game, connecting on 8 passes with a touchdown toss to Travis Benjamin.

The biggest reason for their success that day and the start of the season was the incredibly strong running game. They had a three-headed monster at tailback with veteran Ben Tate, rookie Isaiah Crowell, and rookie Terrance West, and didn't hesitate to use it.

Tate was drafted by the Houston Texans in the second round of the 2010 NFL Draft out of Auburn where he was an absolute stud. His rookie season with Houston never got out of the gate as during the Texans preseason opener in 2010, Tate broke his ankle and was placed on injured reserve. Not much of him was expected heading into 2011 as premier NFL rusher Adrian Foster was their feature back, but even with having to back up Foster and split a portion of the carries, he finished the 2011 regular season with 942 rushing yards on 175 attempts (a 5.4 yards-per-carry average, third-highest in the NFL) with 4 rushing touchdowns and 98 total receiving yards in 15 games played.

In fact, it was during that season that Tate and Foster combined for a franchise record, against who else but the Cleveland Browns. Tate ran for 115 yards against the Cleveland Browns in week 9 while Arian Foster ran for 124 yards in the same contest, leading the Texans to 261 yards on the ground, a franchise record.

After his carries dropped off heavily in 2012 and 2013 as Foster's star continued to rise, Tate wanted out of Houston and got his wish when Tate signed with the Cleveland Browns on March 15, 2014. It was a somewhat under-the-radar signing, but a key one for the Browns as shown that day against Pittsburgh and earlier in the year when on October 5, 2014, he ran for a career-high 123 yards on 22 carries in a 29–28 win over the Tennessee Titans.

Sadly, for Tate, his career as a Brown would only last eight games as Tate was released by the Browns on November 18, 2014. In the weeks leading up to his release, he grew frustrated with the amount of carries he was getting due to the three-back rotation system the Browns had recently employed, giving Tate, Isaiah Crowell, and Terrance West fairly even playing time at running back.

The story of Isaiah Crowell who had a big day that day as well with 77 yards on 12 carries with a touchdown, is a much different story. He was a standout at Carver High School in Georgia; he rushed for 4,872 yards with 61 touchdowns on 429 carries for the Tigers football team. He was considered the best running back recruit by Scout.com and the fourth-best by *Rivals.com*.

After a promising start to his college career at Georgia, things went south for Crowell. On June 29, 2012, Crowell was arrested on possession of a weapon in a school zone, possession of a firearm with an altered identification, and carrying a concealed firearm. Crowell was dismissed from the University of Georgia football team due to his arrest and his constant disciplinary problems—including failing a drug test.

With his back up against the wall, and his chances at the NFL dwindling, he was forced to take a spot on the Alabama State roster where he finished the year with 1,121 yards rushing and 15 touchdowns. Crowell had five 100-yard rushing games in the 2013 season and finished his college career with 2813 yards and 35 touchdowns from his years at Georgia and Alabama State combined. Because of his off-the-field drama at Georgia, Crowell did not get drafted and on May 10, 2014, he signed as an undrafted free agent with the Cleveland Browns.

As the year went on, Crowell would get more and more touches. Crowell played in all 16 games and started 4. He finished his rookie season with 607 rushing yards on 148 attempts and eight touchdowns plus nine receptions for 87 yards. Among rookies, Crowell ranked fifth in rushing yards, only one of 9 rookies to break 500 yards, and one of 5 to break 600 yards. Crowell was ranked second in rushing touchdowns among rookies, just behind Cincinnati Bengals' running back Jeremy Hill.

Crowell would stay in Cleveland though 2017 and had plenty of big games during dark times. Sadly, his failure to stay out of drama off the field caught up to him once again as on July 2016, following the deaths of Alton Sterling and Philando Castile, Crowell posted on his Instagram a controversial violent image of a faceless person dressed in black who was slitting the throat of a captive law enforcement officer with a knife; he later had the photo deleted and apologized for his actions.

The win over Pittsburgh was part of 6 wins in an 8 game stretch, that saw the Browns reach 7–4 by week 11.

## 2019 SEASON WEEK 12
### *Cleveland 21, Pittsburgh 7*
The 2019 Cleveland Browns came into the NFL season with more hype than any team had in many years. After a hot finish to the 2018 season

with rookie quarterback Baker Mayfield, and the free agent signing of dynamic wide receiver Odell Beckham Jr., the expectations for the 2019 Cleveland Browns were through the roof. Mayfield broke rookie passing records in 2018 and was seen as the new face of the franchise; meanwhile, the Steelers and Ravens were supposed to be taking a step back which should have left the division wide open for Cleveland's taking.

There was only one small problem with any of this, and that was someone forgot to tell the Browns they still needed to play the games. Rookie head coach Freddie Kitchens seemed flustered and lost most of the time, and things simply weren't working out headed into this week 12 Thursday Night Football matchup with Pittsburgh.

This was the Browns' fourth venture onto national prime time television that season. A week 2 23–3 win on Monday Night Football in New York over the Jets was followed up by losses to the Rams on Sunday Night of 20–13, and a 31–3 blowout loss in San Francisco to the 49ers. Cold reality hit Cleveland after a week 8 loss to Denver that left them 2–6 and pretty much stunned. That loss came to quarterback Brandon Allen who was making his first ever NFL appearance. Things were that bad.

Now, even at 2–6, the Browns were still hanging on to a glimmer of hope, as crazy as it seemed; an eight-game winning streak didn't seem as crazy as one would think as they were about to face a host of teams with losing records. This included the Bengals and Steelers twice each, the Arizona Cardinals, the Miami Dolphins who all had losing records at the time. Even their week 9 opponent at home versus Buffalo was a winnable game considering the Bills hadn't beaten anyone with a winning record.

It was all in front of the Browns despite the miserable start, and they began taking care of business week 9 by defeating Buffalo in the final seconds on a Baker Mayfield to Hollywood Rashard Higgins touchdown pass. He had been in Freddie Kitchens doghouse most of the season, and was finally let out just in time for Mayfield to find him in the back of the endzone for the win.

This improved the Browns 4–6 and kept them in the conversation as the Steelers rolled into town. The Steelers came in at 5–5 and not the usual fierce opponent with Ben Roethlisberger out once again to injury.

The Browns had a good record against Pittsburgh on national television, and also a great record against Pittsburgh with Big Ben sidelined.

A few plays into the game, Mayfield hit OBJ for a forty-two-yard hook up down to the one-yard line and the nonexistent roof came off First Energy Stadium. It had looked as though OBJ scored and he and Mayfield had horrible chemistry to that point in the season, so it was a much-needed play. The officials reviewed it and called it down and the one-yard line. Despite the buzz of the touchdown to OBJ being gone, Cleveland scored on the very next play with a Mayfield sneak and the Browns were off and running.

Over the next four quarters, the Browns built a 21–7 lead with five minutes left to play with touchdown passes to Jarvis Landry and Stephen Carlson. The game was well in hand but a seemingly ordinary Jamie Gillian punt with 1:47 that gave the Steelers the ball back until this 1:47 proved to be more dramatic than it needed to be. Not so much the punt, but rather, what would happen 93 seconds later would ruin the Cleveland Browns' season. Had the Browns gotten one more first down and simply taken knees to run out the clock, none of what was about to happen would have occurred.

Myles Garrett attended Martin High School in Arlington, Texas, where he was a letterman in football, basketball, and track. In football, he had 19.5 sacks as a senior and was the 2013 recipient of the Landry Award, given to the top high school player in the Dallas-Fort Worth area. He was also rated as a five-star recruit by the *Rivals.com* recruiting network and was ranked as the second-best overall player in his class. He committed to Texas A&M as the number two overall prospect in the nation.

He wasted no time making an impact as an Aggie as he finished his freshman season with 11.5 sacks (second in the SEC), 53 total tackles, 14 tackles for loss, 10 quarterback hurries, and a blocked kick as he was a consensus Freshman All-American and Freshman All-SEC selection. His sophomore season was every bit as good as he recorded 57 total tackles (36 solo), 18.5 tackles for loss, 7 quarterback hurries, 5 forced fumbles, and a blocked punt.

The season earned Garrett a first-team All-American selection by the Walter Camp Football Foundation and the Football Writers Association of America. Garrett was also the Bill Willis Award winner as the top defensive lineman. Garrett recorded 8.5 sacks, 32 total tackles (18 of them solo), 15.0 tackles for loss, 10 quarterback hurries, 2 forced fumbles, and a pass breakup.

The Browns had whiffed on fellow Texas A&M Aggie Johnny Manziel in the 2014 NFL Draft, but that didn't scare them away from using their top pick on Garrett in the 2017 NFL Draft. Garrett attended the NFL Scouting Combine in Indianapolis and solidified his position as a top ten pick with an impressive combine performance. His 41" vertical jump was the top performance of all defensive linemen and he also finished with the second-best performance in the bench press and broad jump. Garrett also had the third fastest forty-yard dash of all defensive linemen at the combine, which highly impressed scouts due to his size.

On March 30, 2017, Garrett attended Texas A&M's Pro Day and chose to perform the 40-yard dash (4.65s), 20-yard dash (2.71), 10-yard dash (1.57s), and broad jump (10'6"). The Browns went 1–15 in 2016; they badly needed a difference maker on defense, and Garrett could've been just the guy for them. That's why it came as no surprise when the Cleveland Browns selected Garrett with the first overall pick of the 2017 NFL Draft.

The Browns' debut of Garrett would have to wait, however, as he suffered a high ankle sprain getting ready for the first game of the season. Garrett wouldn't actually make his debut until October 8 against the New York Jets, and sacked Josh McCown twice, including once on his first-ever NFL play. He got off to a hot start with four sacks in his first three games, but then a concussion would sideline him again.

Overall, for the 2017 season, Garrett recorded 31 combined tackles (19 solo), 7 sacks, 1 forced fumble, 1 pass defense, and 1 fumble recovery during his rookie season. Due to injury he only played 11 of 16 games, but still finished first on the team in sacks. The year was a nightmare for the Browns however as they became only the second team in NFL history next to the 2008 Detroit Lions to finish 0–16.

Heading into his second year in the NFL, the talk about Garrett was that he was possibly injury prone and needed a full 16-game season to show everyone what he could do. In the 2018 season, Garrett started all 16 games and recorded 13.5 sacks, 44 combined tackles, 12 tackles-for-loss, 29 quarterback hits, 3 passes defensed, and 3 forced fumbles. His 13.5 sacks ranked sixth in the NFL that year. The Browns won 7 games, he was great, and the pick now felt justified.

Starting with the 2019 season, however, things about the "gentle giant" seemed to be changing. He started training MMA with Stipe Miocic and developed a bit of a tougher edge. All of this gave a nastier and even scarier feel to him. His sack totals were climbing fast as well with two sacks in the opener against the Tennessee Titans and then three against the New York Jets.

The issue in those two games was the NFL felt he was "too aggressive." Garrett was fined a combined $52,639 for three fouls, a face mask hit on Delanie Walker as well as the two roughing the passer fouls on Trevor Siemian, the second of which resulted in Siemian tearing his anterior cruciate ligament. He was better than ever, but at the same time, on the radar of every official out there.

Despite all of this, he was seen as calm as they come. He was massive, but he was the kind of guy who was constantly giving back to charity and never in the middle of any drama or controversy. He was the perfect player with the ideal mental attitude. Garrett was everything Cleveland Browns fans loved and the kind of guy who fans would root for on Sundays, and then be more than fine with letting their kids watch on Mondays. He was constantly being double teamed and held on every single play, and never complained.

All of this made what was about to happen more stunning that anyone could ever imagine as we return to the Thursday night Pittsburgh game with Cleveland up 21–7 and the game in the bag with fourteen seconds left. Garrett pulled Steelers quarterback Mason Rudolph to the ground following a late hit. Upset by the late hit, Rudolph started to attack Garrett by kicking him in the groin and attempting to pull off Garrett's helmet. After getting back up, Garrett forcibly removed Rudolph's helmet as

Steelers offensive linemen Maurkice Pouncey and David DeCastro tried to hold back Garrett.

Garrett then violently swung Rudolph's own helmet at him, striking him in the head with the underside of the helmet. A fight ensued that resulted in Garrett, Pouncey, and Browns defensive tackle Larry Ogunjobi being ejected; Pouncey punched and kicked Garrett's head several times after the strike, while Ogunjobi pushed a helmetless Rudolph to the ground as he stood watching the fight.

The next day, the NFL suspended Garrett indefinitely, and at a minimum for the remainder of the 2019 season. He was also fined $45,623 while Rudolph was fined $50,000. Thirty-three other players were fined $3,000 for entering a fight zone, and the Browns and Steelers organizations were fined $250,000 each. Garrett appealed his suspension on November 20, but the suspension was upheld.

Garrett would go on to become the all-time sack leader in Cleveland Browns history. He is still a pillar of the community and the face of the defense week in and week out. Making matters worse when you go back and soak everything in, the Steelers called a timeout to run that useless play from their own 17-yard line on a third and 29. All of it wasn't even needed, and then you start to question why in the world Myles Garrett was on the field for that play in a game that was over anyway? All of this among other things led to the firing of Cleveland Browns head coach Freddie Kitchens.

Despite the wild ending, the bottom line was the Browns beat the Steelers once again on a Thursday night and continued to gain confidence that they could beat their rivals.

## 2022 SEASON, WEEK 3
### *Cleveland 29, Pittsburgh 27*

We spoke about both major wins over Pittsburgh in 2020 that led to the playoffs, stopped the Hines Field Streak, and won the first playoff game in the new era of the Cleveland Browns franchise. You can read more about those in chapter 9.

With that being said, I wanted to jump ahead and finish with week 3 of the 2022 season. The Browns were coming off a stunning loss to the

New York Jets 31–30 the previous Sunday in which the Browns blew a thirteen-point lead with less than a minute to go in the game as the Jets got two touchdowns and converted an onside kick to win. They would have to bounce back quickly as Pittsburgh was coming to First Energy Stadium just four days later for a prime time showcase.

The Browns used a steady diet of Amari Cooper, Nick Chubb, and David Njoku en route to a 29–17 victory over their rival the Pittsburgh Steelers tonight to improve to 2–1 on the season. The special teams were a bit shaky again, and so was the secondary, but all in all, the Browns looked good in the win.

Amari Cooper looked open all night: he wreaked havoc on the Pittsburgh defense as he caught 7 balls for 101 yards, and a touchdown. David Njoku was being counted on hard that season with the extreme lack of wide receiver depth for the Browns; he stepped up with 9 catches for 89 yards and a score.

Brissett easily had his best game as a Cleveland Brown using the above weapons around him. The signal caller went 21 of 31 for 220 yards and 2 touchdowns. He also rushed the ball 3 times for 11 yards, all of which were for first downs in third and fourth and short situations.

The tandem of Nick Chubb and Kareem Hunt once again went to work early and often in the victory. Nick Chubb rushed for 113 yards on 22 touchdowns with the score. Hunt went for 47 yards on the ground on 12 carries. Together, they went for over 150 yards on the ground along with Hunt catching 3 balls for 14 yards.

Pittsburgh fans would get on their Kenny Pickett bandwagon shortly after, but quite frankly, Trubisky played well enough for the Steelers to win once again. Mitch went 19 of 31 for 209 yards with a rushing touchdown. It is not his fault they were losing; there were several dropped passes and the Browns held Najee Harris to just 56 yards on the ground.

Late into the first quarter, the Browns used a 7 play, 61-yard drive to score first. The drive was capped off by a Brissett to Cooper 11-yard touchdown pass. The Browns took advantage of a shorter field following the Chris Boswell field goal miss. They took advantage of a good break, and that is what winning teams do.

Najee Harris got the Steelers on the board on the first play of the second quarter. Pittsburgh ran a quick tempo no huddle drive to move 7 plays in 3 minutes, covering 75 yards. This followed the Browns score that resulted in a touchback.

The Browns, as they did for the bulk of the night, answered the Steeler score with one of their own. Brissett used an empty backfield set to his advantage for quick pass plays, most of which going to Njoku who had the touchdown catch on this drive. This time, he found his tight end from 7 yards out to put the Browns back ahead. Cade York promptly missed the extra point as the Browns fans held their breath.

The Steelers, once again, wasted no time responding as they cruised down the field by moving 75 yards in 10 plays to go up 14–13 on the Mitch Trubisky 1-yard scramble. This gave the hometown boy a reason to celebrate in front of his family and friends in the crowd.

It looked for a moment like the Browns would take the lead before half on a field goal in the two-minute drill. However, Kevin Stefanski elected to go for it on fourth and two. The pass to Cooper was just a bit off. At first, it looked as though he caught it as it was called a first down, but then the review gave it back to Pittsburgh on the incomplete pass.

The Steelers were unable to take advantage with a two-minute drill of their own, and had to settle for the 14–13 lead at half. The third quarter saw very little scoring, but again, the Browns used smart play calling to convert third and fourth and shorts, before eventually settling for a thirty-four-yard field goal from York to give them the lead at 16–14 in the closing moments of the third quarter.

Up two points to start the fourth quarter, the Browns went back to work with a dink and dunk system that allowed them to move the ball 80 yards in 11 plays, while soaking up 6:35 off the game clock. They cashed in with a Nick Chubb 1-yard touchdown on a dramatic fourth and four call. York made it interesting, but did convert the extra point to extend the Browns lead to 23–14 with 9:33 to play.

After a 35-yard Chris Boswell field goal made it 23–17 with 1:51 to play, it was another onside kick situation for the Browns to try and recover to ice the game. The Browns managed to recover it this week, and ice the victory.

When the Cleveland Browns officially left for Baltimore in the early part of 1996, a little piece of die-hard fans everywhere died. They had to sit back and watch Baltimore announce a new name, new colors, logo, all of it! In hindsight, it was a blessing that Baltimore had to start from scratch with new colors, logo, name, and so on because the only place for the Browns was and is Cleveland.

Also easing the blow, just a bit, was the fact that the Ravens were lousy the three years the Browns were gone. In their first three years in Baltimore, they had a combined record of 16–31–1 in a disastrous run with the Ravens. Head coach Ted Marchibroda never stood a chance as the once "old Browns" had the talent, but it just seemed like it took them forever to get adjusted to being somewhere new as the seasons of losses piled up.

Their first year in the NFL, the Ravens won an emotional opening week game 19–14 with a dramatic last second Earnest Byner touchdown run. Just how ironic is that? However, after the opening week victory, the rest of the season was a nightmare as the Ravens finished 4–12. Things didn't get much better in 1997 and 1998 with 6 wins during each campaign.

The story of Marchibroda in Baltimore was supposed to be a feel-good legacy-type tale. Marchibroda's first head coaching appointment was with the Baltimore Colts beginning on January 15, 1975, after spending years in Washington as an offensive coordinator. He took over a team that went 2–12 and was one of the two worst in the NFL in 1974.

He was up for the challenge and led one of the two biggest turnarounds in pro football history when the Colts ended the 1975 regular season at 10–4 and qualified for the playoffs by winning the AFC East title for the first of three consecutive years. All three postseason appearances ended in divisional round losses, first to the Steelers in both 1975 and 1976 and the Oakland Raiders in 1977.

Despite his early success, it wouldn't last long. His five years as Colts head coach concluded with a pair of 5–11 last-place finishes in 1978 and 1979. Marchibroda was fired on December 27, 1979, by Jim Irsay who was getting ready to sneak the Colts off to Indianapolis soon enough.

Oddly enough, he got a second chance at being a head coach and it just happened to be in Indianapolis. Marchibroda led the Colts to a 9–7 record in 1992. Three seasons later, the team fell one play short of Super Bowl XXX when it lost the 1995 AFC Championship Game to the Steelers, but the playoff run did not guarantee job security for Marchibroda who parted ways with the Colts on February 9, 1996, after his demand for a contract extension of two years rather than one was rejected.

With that being said, the return of football to Baltimore in 1996 meant the return of Marchibroda as Art Model was trying hard to sell a feel-good story. The third time would not be the charm and his stay was short. Marchibroda was notified that he was not going to be retained on December 28, 1998.

Now, if losing the Browns to Baltimore wasn't bad enough, they also took the one man the new Browns coveted to be their first head coach of the new era, Brian Billick. Coach Billick had a tremendous run on the coaching staff of the Minnesota Vikings. Billick was hired as an assistant coach by the Vikings. The Vikings made the playoffs during six of the seven seasons (1992–1998) that Billick spent with the team, and set several offensive records in the process. In 1998, Minnesota set an NFL record for most points scored in a season (556). Not only that, but they set a team record with forty-one touchdown passes with most of them coming from aged veteran Randall Cunningham who hadn't been relative in years.

Although Billick had the opportunity to interview for the head coaching job of the reactivated Cleveland Browns and was rumored to be their top candidate, he chose to interview with the Ravens first and never left Baltimore. The hiring of Billick proved to be genius and increase the pain for Cleveland fans as he went 85–67 in nine seasons (1999–2007) with the team, including 5–3 in the playoffs. He won a Super Bowl title in Super Bowl XXXV over the New York Giants. All of this and more gave Cleveland fans reasons to hate Baltimore.

The first year back in the league, the Browns lost both games to the 8–8 Ravens by scores of 17–10 in Cleveland and 41–9 in Baltimore. The Ravens defeated Cleveland twice again in 2000, but that's understandable as many teams lost to Baltimore in 2000.

The next season, the Ravens finished with a 12–4 record and earned their first playoff berth. The Ravens took advantage of their vaunted defense, which allowed an NFL record-low 165 points in the regular season (for a point differential of 168; the Ravens also led the league in turnover differential at +23) during the playoffs to advance to Super Bowl XXXV against the New York Giants. It was a blowout 34–7 victory, giving Billick his first and only Super Bowl.

Heading into the 2001 season, the Browns were 0–4 in the rivalry and bound to turn things around with new head coach Butch Davis. It was this season that Cleveland began a yearly tradition of defeating the defending Super Bowl Champions, and it began week 6 as the 3–2 Browns hosted Baltimore.

## 2001 SEASON WEEK 6
### *Cleveland 24, Baltimore 14*
*"Defeating the Old Browns"*

The Browns used a tremendous day passing from Tim Couch who went 11 of 18 for 149 yards and two touchdowns to lead his team to the franchise's first win over their newest rivals. The touchdown passes went the way of Kevin Johnson and Quincy Morgan. Also cashing in for the Browns was tailback James Jackson with seventy-seven yards rushing and a score as the Browns built a 24–6 lead at one point.

The defense showed up and showed out, as they combined to pick off Ravens quarterback Elvis Grbac twice. The decision to get rid of Super Bowl winning quarterback Trent Dilfer for Grbac was much maligned in Baltimore. The front office thought with the defense they had in 2000, that their Super Bowl win had nothing to do with Dilfer so they cut ties with him for Grbac. Six weeks in, it already wasn't working out and they replaced him during the Browns game with Randall Cunningham whom Billick tried and failed to capture magic with yet again.

The win moved the Cleveland Browns to an improbable 4–2, by far the best start of their three seasons in the NFL. They would go on to drop their next two games in overtime to Chicago 27–21 and Pittsburgh 15–12, both in heartbreaking fashion before traveling to Baltimore for a week 9 rematch.

## 2001 SEASON WEEK 9 AT BALTIMORE
### *Cleveland 27, Baltimore 17*
*"The Legend of Ben Gay"*

This game was truly bizarre and it was only appropriate that it featured the Cleveland Browns enigma known as Ben Gay. In the 2001 Cleveland Browns training camp, the lack of a running game was one of the first things on their list to correct. They had Jamel White and drafted James Jackson who would combine for 997 rushing yards in 2001. Neither was a stud, but they hoped to get by with the combination of both.

Then, there was this enigma known as "Ben Gay" who was in camp with the Browns. His path to Cleveland was a riches-to-rags story; yes, you just read that correctly. Gay was a star running back at Spring High School in Spring, Texas. As a senior in 1997, he was a *USA Today* first-team All-American.

He was so respected coming out of high school, he could have played and started as a freshman anywhere in the country; he chose Baylor over Florida, Florida State, and Miami. It looked like it would be cannot-miss for Gay, then he missed. Five weeks into his freshman season in 1998, he was kicked off the team for rules violations.

He eventually enrolled at Garden City Community College. Playing 9 games in 1999, he rushed for 1,442 yards and 17 touchdowns but was dismissed from the team because of his grades and rules violations. He went from playing for a BIG 12 Division 1 college to taking a job bouncing at a bar after community college.

He was signed by the Edmonton Eskimos out of college, but left Canada after only a few short months after he was signed by the Cleveland Browns in July of 2001, right before camp was set to start. He was brought in to help with kick returning, and did just that as he returned a kick in all 16 regular season games for 513 yards on 23 total returns.

The problem with Gay that kept him out of the backfield was his lack of ability to hold on to the ball when handed off to him. He fumbled 4 times in only 51 carries. That works out to fumbling the ball every 12 times you carry it. That is a good way to play yourself out of the NFL which is exactly what he did. The fumbling, off-the-field antics which continued, and then simply bizarre behaviors in the locker room and meetings, jettisoned Gay not only from the Browns, but the NFL in general after just one season in Cleveland. He never played in the NFL again, and his life was out of control for nearly the next decade's worth of problems.

However, for his one brief flash in Cleveland, he looked like the second coming of "Jim" himself Brown. After he tore off a fifty-eight-yard run in the Browns' first scrimmage, fans took note and would chant his name whenever he took the field. It was with the momentum, hype, and quite frankly, necessity that he was forced into a starting role when the Browns traveled to Baltimore.

With James Jackson on the sidelines injured, they had to go to Gay to back up Jamel White and he cashed in with 54 yards on 18 carries and scored once. A decent day, nothing great, but fans were in love with him because the Browns beat their newest rivals for the second time that season, in their house!

While fans and some media focused on Gay's big day, the real story was the seven combined interceptions thrown by Tim Couch and Ravens starter Elvis Grbac that afternoon. The Browns defense was the true reason for their growth in 2001 and in this game as they picked off the Northeast Ohio-born Grbac four times.

As for Gay, his rocket came plummeting back to earth the next week in an 18–0 victory over Cincinnati. Gay was held to 16 yards on 10 attempts. Between his lousy day, and Couch being picked off two more times, it was even more evident that the Browns 6–4 start may have been a fraud, and it was, as they would go on to finish the season 7–9 and Ben Gay was never heard from again.

## 2002 SEASON, WEEK 15 IN BALTIMORE
### *Cleveland 14, Baltimore 13*
*"Must Win"*

The Browns lost a heartbreaker on prime time Sunday night television earlier in the year in front of a sold-out crowd to the Ravens. A miraculous Kelly Holcomb-led comeback fell just short and the Browns dropped to 2–3. Since that Sunday night however, the Browns went 5–2 and still had a chance at the playoffs sitting at 7–7 headed to Baltimore for the rematch. The Browns chances were extremely slim, but they knew as long as they won in Baltimore, they wouldn't be eliminated and would have a chance for a miracle finish week 16.

The game was not fun to watch; in fact, it was downright boring, but the Browns managed to pull off a shaky 14–13 win. Cleveland scored a touchdown on their first drive of the game with a Jamel White three-yard rush, and then on the last drive of the game with a one-yard touchdown toss from Tim Couch to Mark Campbell. They did absolutely nothing between those drives the other fifty-plus minutes of the game, but it turned out not to even matter.

The Browns defense was once again stout in the win, holding the Ravens to a pair of field goals from Matt Stover and a touchdown pass from now starting quarterback Jeff Blake to Travis Taylor. The only dark spot for Cleveland was them allowing Ravens running back Jamal Lewis to put up 100 yards on them. A win is a win however, and the following week's dramatic win over Atlanta would lead to the Browns making the postseason.

## 2004 Season, Week 1
### Cleveland 20, Baltimore 3
*"A Rare Win on Opening Day"*

With all the things that have gone wrong for the Browns over the last twenty-plus years—draft pick busts, ownership switches, coaching switches, GMs disappearing in the middle of the night or sending nasty emails to fans, star players never working out, and just the craziest things one could imagine actually happening, up to and including a ref tossing a flag in your offensive lineman's eyeball (causing him to have to retire)—all of it has been more horrible than anyone's worst possible fear, but what keeps fans coming back each season? Simple: each year starts a new with opening day when their record is 0–0 all over again.

Sadly, for the Browns, that has been probably the biggest black-and-blue eye ever. Since their return to the league in 1999, through the start of the 2022 season, they had only won twice on opening day. They've gone 2–21–1 on opening day. Again, it almost doesn't seem real.

Even with that all being said, no one forgets their first time, and that is where this game comes into play.

After making the playoffs in 2002, the 2003 season was a disaster and the Browns were desperate to start anew. They brought in Jeff Garcia to play quarterback, cut Tim Couch, and drafted the high-profile tight end Kellen Winslow Jr. out of The University of Miami. The hype was real for Cleveland and the hopes were high as they welcomed in the Baltimore Ravens to start the 2004 regular season.

The very first play of the game was a very simple off-tackle William Green run for a one-yard. The play went nowhere but when the Cleveland fullback drove Ray Lewis into the ground like a nail and then stood over him, Cleveland fans knew this game would be different. The Browns had attitude and would fear no one on this day!

Again, it wasn't pretty as Cleveland only had ten first downs the entire game, and only led 3–0 at the half, but it simply didn't matter as a win is a win. By the end of the game, it was put away comfortably as the Browns led 20–3 with 4:20 left to play, and fans everywhere spent that time celebrating. A win has never felt so good week 1 as that one did!

Jeff Garcia went 15 of 24 passing for 180 yards with a 46-yard touchdown strike to Quincy Morgan. He also had a long connection of 51 yards to Andrew Davis. Garcia also rushed for a touchdown in the win as well as the Browns started the season with a win for the first time in the franchise's new history.

## 2005 SEASON, WEEK 16 IN CLEVELAND
### Cleveland 20, Baltimore 16
*"The Comeback Kid Closes Out in Style"*

The Browns played in exactly thirty games since their 2004 opening week victory in Cleveland over Baltimore and their 2005 season finale back at home versus Baltimore. They went 8–22 in those games, switching from Head Coach Butch Davis to Romeo Crennel and switching from starting quarterback Jeff Garcia to Charlie Frye. They had nothing but pride to play for as they stood at 5–10 welcoming 6–9 Baltimore to town.

The Ravens led 13–0 and then 13–6 at halftime after a pair of Phil Dawson field goals. Two weeks earlier, the Browns had used a second half comeback to defeat the Raiders in Oakland 9–7, and looked to do it again. Fans were slowly gaining faith in rookie Charlie Frye, and if he could lead the Browns back again, it would give them a ton of momentum heading into the 2006 season.

Frye did just that as the Browns outscored the Ravens 14–3 in the second half. The Ravens actually struck first on another Matt Stover Field Goal, his third, before Frye took over. The Akron native would connect on a touchdown pass to Antonio Bryant to cut the lead to 16–13 and give the Browns the spark they needed. Later on, it was Dennis Northcutt returning a punt 62 yards to the house to give the Browns a 20–16 win.

Both of the Cleveland Browns wins over Baltimore during the 10–6 2007 season, including the Phil Dawson double doink, are recapped in that chapter.

## 2013 SEASON, WEEK 9
### *Cleveland 24, Baltimore 18*
*"Staying in Contention"*

We spoke a bit about this season in the prime time chapter as Cleveland used the shocking surge of momentum from Brian Hoyer to jump out to a 3–2 record on the season. Sadly, Hoyer got hurt, and the Browns promptly lost three straight to Detroit, Green Bay, and Kansas City to fall to 3–5. They actually led the Detroit game 17–7 at home, before allowing twenty-four straight Detroit points in the second half as the wheels fell off.

Now, at 3–5, the playoffs were looking bleak, but a win over Baltimore could place them right back in the picture for the Division. No one had separated them from the pack as of yet, and the Ravens were struggling, coming to town 3–4. They would follow this game up with a bye, and then games versus Pittsburgh and Cincinnati, so it was all right in front of them if they could win.

With Hoyer done for the year, and Brandon Weeden being a bigger question mark than ever, they had no choice but to insert Jason Campbell one more time and see if they could catch lightning in a bottle from the journeyman backup. Campbell answered the bell with 3 touchdown passes on 23 of 35 passing with 262 yards and no picks. His biggest threat was Greg Little with 7 catches for 122 yards and Josh Gordon with 3 catches for 44 yards. Remarkably, 2 of the 3 touchdown passes went to Davone Bess who come to Cleveland from Miami with a lot of promise, but never quite figured it out in Cleveland.

Bess was extremely good in Miami as he caught over 50 balls a year, and had over 500 yards a year as a solid producer for the Dolphins. No one is quite sure what happened, but Bess never panned out as he only started 3 games for the Browns, and never played again after the 2013 season in Cleveland.

It should be noted as well that this was the season after Baltimore won the Super Bowl. So, this was yet another season in which the Browns came out and beat the defending Super Bowl Champions as they did in 2008 with the New York Giants, 2009 against Pittsburgh, and 2010 against the New Orleans Saints.

This win was also special because it would be the last for the Cleveland Browns under head coach Rob Chudzinski as they finished the season with seven straight losses to end the year at 4–12. Coach "Chud" was gone at year's end and the next revamp of Cleveland Browns football would start soon enough.

## 2015 SEASON, WEEK 5 IN BALTIMORE
### Cleveland 33, Baltimore 30
*"The Record Breaker"*

By week 5 of the 2015 season, a few things were clear: the Johnny Manziel experiment wasn't going to work out, and the Browns were going to be light-years away from being competitive. As much as they tried to give Manziel a chance to get some work in, he simply couldn't stay out of trouble so they went to the guy they hoped would at least keep them in games and maybe sneak out a few—enter Josh McCown.

Manziel started game two of the 2015 season after McCown got hurt game one against the Jets, and led the Browns to a 28–14 victory over Tennessee with two long touchdown passes to Travis Benjamin in the win of 60 and 50 yards. It appeared they would stay with Manziel

158

and give him the chance to shine, but he promptly got in trouble, and benched yet again.

McCown was ready for game 3 of the season, and threw for 341 yards on 28 of 49 passing with 2 touchdowns in a hard fought 27–20 loss. He nearly led them back from a 27–10 fourth quarter deficit. From there, he threw for 356 more yards in a heartbreaking 30–27 walkoff field goal loss in San Diego. The Browns may have been 0–3 with him as the starter, but he was tearing it up as they traveled to Baltimore for the week 5 clash.

On February 27, 2015, McCown signed a three-year contract worth $14 million with the Cleveland Browns. To this point in his career, he played for and started games with Arizona, Detroit, Oakland, Carolina, Chicago, and Tampa Bay. He never had more than thirteen touchdown passes in a single season, thus the Browns weren't expecting much but hopefully enough to mold Manziel and lead the Browns. This fateful day in Baltimore, he did much more than that as he threw for 356 yards and 2 touchdowns against the San Diego Chargers but the Browns lost by a score of 30–27. In a 33–30 overtime victory over the Baltimore Ravens in week 5, he set a new career high and the Browns record for passing yards in a regular season game with 457 as the Browns moved to 2–3 while McCown was named the AFC Offensive Player of the Week.

It was the Browns' first win in Baltimore since 2007 and McCown also became the first player in NFL history to record more than 450 passing yards, two passing touchdowns, a rushing touchdown, and no interceptions in one game. He was also the first player in Browns history to pass for more than 300 yards in three straight games and his 1,154 yards set a record for most in a three-game span in franchise history, surpassing the former record of 1,038 set by Brian Sipe in 1980.

McCown finished the season having played in just 8 games, but threw for a ridiculous 2,109 yards in that short stretch, with 12 touchdowns and only 4 interceptions. If you average that out over a 16-game season, that is 4,000-plus yards. Injuries and constant drama ruined his brief stay in Cleveland.

Also, very important to note on the record-setting day was the fact that none of his traditional receivers had 100 yards in the win. In fact, his top receiver that day was a tight end named Gary Barnidge who caught 8 balls for 139 yards. Also, in a 457-yard game, he only had 2 touchdowns in the air as placekicker Travis Coon nailed 4 field goals.

## 2019 SEASON WEEK 5
### Cleveland 40, Baltimore 18

All three phases of the Cleveland Browns team played well and it led to a dominant 40–25 victory in Baltimore. The win moved the Browns into a tie for first place with the Ravens who were also at 2–2 in what appeared to be a two-team race in the AFC North.

The Browns needed to establish a run game and also force turnovers on defense if they were going to be successful, and they did exactly that. Nick Chubb finished with a big day, tallying up 165 yards on 20 carries, also scoring 3 times. The Browns' defense forced three turnovers and held Baltimore to a season low in yards from scrimmage.

Baker Mayfield took a lot of heat that week from several media outlets, and also other players around the league. He didn't let it affect him as he too had his best effort of the young season. Mayfield went 20 of 30 passing for 342 yards and a touchdown. He also threw an interception on a route in which Jarvis Landry gave up on.

We can't be too hard on Landry, however, as he had a monster day. Landry finished with 167 yards on 8 catches, but did leave the game with a concussion. The biggest reason behind the Browns win and perhaps the most encouraging sign of early 2019 was that they answered every Ravens score almost immediately.

Down 7–0 with 1:55 to go in the first half, the Ravens' Lamar Jackson hit Miles Boykin in the back of the endzone, wide open to tie the game.

The Browns would not fold, and instead answered right away with a great two-minute drive. They even converted a fourth and short. They would have to settle for a field goal, but it was still a promising sign as they led 10–7 at the half.

The trend of answering Ravens scores continued in the second half. After the Ravens started the third quarter by tying the game with a field goal, the Browns wasted no time in getting the lead back.

A slick 59-yard launch to Ricky Seals Jones would set up the 14-yard Nick Chubb touchdown run to give the Browns a 17–10 lead. The

Browns would build on that lead as the quarter came to a close with another Nick Chubb touchdown run. This time from 2 yards to make it 24–10 as the quarter ended.

The Ravens struck quickly in the fourth quarter and also converted a two-point conversion to make it 24–18. Before anyone could get nervous about the lead only being 6 points, the Browns once again showed incredible heart and determination by answering the touchdown with one of their own immediately.

A thunderous 88-yard touchdown sprint by Nick Chubb took the wind out of the Ravens' sails and all but sealed up the victory. At 30–18, the lead was only 12 points, but the momentum was clearly with the Brown and Orange. Mayfield and the Browns would not take their foot off the gas, forcing another Ravens turnover, and converting it into points.

The Browns built the lead to 40–18 with under two minutes to play, as Ravens fans headed for the exits. The Browns never trailed in the game. The Browns also won the turnover battle 3–1. OBJ only had 2 catches for 20 yards and the Browns still dominated on the road.

# Bonus Chapter

## *The GOAT*

We may have alluded to some of his past in the last chapter, but no one who watched him play or has studied the tapes can ever argue that Jim Brown isn't the greatest athlete to ever play running back in the NFL.

He was a polarizing figure who was loved by many, but hated by some because of his off-the-field persona. Whether you loved him or hated him, everyone who watched him play would agree that he was easily one of the greatest players to ever play the game. He was one of the greatest pure athletes the NFL has ever seen, and could have played in any generation and still dominated.

During his time in the NFL with the Browns, he made the Pro Bowl every year and was named one of the best players in football, if not the very best, eight of nine seasons by the NFL. The AP voted him their Most Valuable Player three times during his career.

For Brown, he had athleticism in his blood from day one as his father was professional boxer Swinton Brown. He was raised by his grandmother, however, where he excelled at all youth sports growing up.

He enrolled to play football and lacrosse at Syracuse University in 1953. He would make an impact his sophomore year with the Orangemen as he was second on the team in rushing, and starting to catch the coaching staff's eyes. It was in his junior year that he put himself on the national map with 676 yards, an average of 5.2 per carry.

In his senior year of 1956, Brown was a consensus first-team All-American. He finished fifth in the Heisman Trophy voting and set school records for highest season rush average (6.2) and most rushing touchdowns in a single game (6). He ran for 986 yards which was third-most in the country despite Syracuse playing in only eight games. He made the most of it in those 8 games, averaging over 100 yards per game and scoring 14 touchdowns. Brown was just getting started.

He saved his best for last as in his final regular season collegiate game, he ran for 197 yards in a 61–7 blowout of Colgate. He scored 6 touchdowns in the game and topped it off by kicking 7 extra points for a school record 43-point game. He was putting up basketball numbers on the football field!

He then went even further in the Cotton Bowl that year versus TCU when he singlehandedly kept them in the game. Against the Horned Frogs, Brown rushed for 132 yards, scored 3 touchdowns, and kicked 3 extra points. Had it not been for a freak blocked punt, TCU would have not scraped by with a 28–27 shocking win.

As mentioned prior, he was a natural-born athlete and could have gone pro in any sport of his choosing. He was that gifted and had unlimited potential. In the 1950s, things were drastically different and college athletes would play multiple sports and stay in college all four years. Brown was the perfect example of that: while at Syracuse he excelled in basketball, track, and especially lacrosse.

Averaging 15 points per game as a sophomore, he was the second-leading scorer for the basketball team. Later that spring, he took to the track where he earned a letter on the track team. In 1955, he finished in fifth place in the National Championship decathlon. His junior year after another dominating year on the football field, he kept it up on the basketball court; he averaged 11.3 points in basketball, and then added lacrosse to his showcase of talents as he was named a second-team All-American in lacrosse.

It was at this point that it was becoming crystal clear that his two best sports were lacrosse and football and he would have his choice of which one to go professional with. His senior year, he was named a first-team All-American in lacrosse (43 goals in 10 games to rank second in scoring nationally). If his growing legend wasn't already enough, his mystique as a superhero would get even bigger when Brown was so dominant in the game that lacrosse rules were changed requiring a lacrosse player to keep their stick in constant motion when carrying the ball (instead of holding it close to his body).

At Syracuse Campus, their lacrosse field has a dome known as JMA Wireless Dome which has an 800-square-foot tapestry depicting Brown in football and lacrosse uniforms with the words "Greatest Player Ever." It's pretty wild to think a man known for his historic career on the football field could have easily had a bigger one in lacrosse.

The Cleveland Browns selected him with the sixth overall pick in the 1957 NFL Draft. This draft also included NFL Hall of Famers such as Len Dawson who went fifth overall to the Pittsburgh Steelers and Paul Hornung first overall to the Green Bay Packers. A few picks after Brown, the Baltimore Colts selected future Hall of Famer Jim Parker. In the third round Tommy McDonald was selected by the Philadelphia Eagles and in the fourth round it was Sonny Jurgensen also going to the Eagles.

Before the draft could conclude, the Cleveland Browns would also select Hall of Famers Henry Jordan in the fifth round and Gene Hickerson in the seventh round. All in all, the NFL Draft that year saw nine total Hall of Famers selected, none bigger than Brown.

Brown wasted no time making an immediate impact as a Cleveland Brown. In just his ninth professional game he went for a career-high 237 yards against the Los Angeles Rams, a team Cleveland fans knew well as they used to be the Cleveland Rams before leaving in 1945 after winning the AAFC Championship. The 237 yards set an NFL single-game record that went unsurpassed for 14 years. It was also a rookie record that stood until Adrian Peterson broke it in 2007 with a single game total of 296 yards against San Diego Chargers.

During his time with the Cleveland Browns, they won the NFL championship in 1964, and were runners-up in 1957 and 1965. In the 1964 championship game, Brown rushed 27 times for 114 yards and caught 3 passes for 37 in the win. A championship that stood as the city's last one until the Cleveland Cavaliers won the NBA Championship in 2016 to end the 52-year drought.

Brown was in the prime of his career but many off-the-field issues and distractions caused much turmoil for the young man as well. Many teammates and fans blamed him for the firing of Paul Brown once Art Modell bought the team.

Once Brown started to taste his first bit of fame outside of the playing field, it was all over as he stepped away from the game forever. Jim Brown shockingly retired from professional football while on the set of *The Dirty Dozen*. This news shook the world of sports and many fans and media members alike didn't believe, figuring it was a power move for Brown. To his credit, however, he held true to his word and never returned to play.

His sensational professional football career led to his induction into the Pro Football Hall of Fame in 1971. His football accomplishments at Syracuse garnered him a berth in the College Football Hall of Fame. Not only that, but because of what he did at Syracuse before turning pro, Brown also earned a spot in the Lacrosse Hall of Fame.

To this day in 2022, he currently holds NFL records for:

- most games with 24 or more points in a career (6)
- highest career touchdowns per game average (1.068)
- most career games with three or more touchdowns (14)
- most games with four or more touchdowns in a career (6)
- most seasons leading the league in rushing attempts (6)
- most seasons leading the league in rushing yards (8)
- highest career rushing yards-per-game average (104.3)
- most seasons leading the league in touchdowns (5)
- most seasons leading the league in yards from scrimmage (6)
- highest average yards from scrimmage per game in a career (125.52)
- most seasons leading the league in combined net yards (5).

Some of those records can be broken, most will never be touched! The amazing thing is as time went on, the legend of Jim Brown got even bigger because no one came close to matching what he did in the short time it took him to do it. In 2002, *The Sporting News* selected him as the greatest football player of all time. On November 4, 2010, Brown was chosen by NFL Network's NFL Films production *The Top 100: NFL's Greatest Players* as the second-greatest player in NFL history, behind only Jerry Rice. In November 2019, he was selected as one of the twelve running backs on the NFL 100th Anniversary All-Time Team. On January 13, 2020, Brown was named the greatest college football player of all time by ESPN, during a ceremony at the College Football Playoff National Championship Game celebrating the 150th anniversary of college football.

Once out of football, he continued to film movies and do everything he could to help grow his rising star in Hollywood even further. Some choices, however, were quite controversial and questioned by many. One of which was his decision to pose nude for the September 1974 issue of *Playgirl* magazine, and is one of the rare celebrities to allow full-frontal nude pictures to be used.

When not posing for magazines, he did his best to try and stay around sports where he could, but the problem was he wasn't very good. In 1965, Brown was the first black televised boxing announcer when he announced a televised boxing match in the United States, for the Terrell–Chuvalo fight. He didn't get many boxing gigs after that. He would eventually try his hand at announcing MMA but it didn't go much better as he was let go after UFC 6.

In 1983, seventeen years after retiring from professional football, Brown teased wishful fans with the crazy notion of coming out of retirement to play for the Los Angeles Raiders when it appeared that Pittsburgh Steelers running back Franco Harris would break Brown's all-time rushing record. Brown didn't like Harris and said his was the style of a coward, running away from tacklers while Brown went right at them. Eventually, Walter Payton of the Chicago Bears broke the record on October 7, 1984, with Brown having ended thoughts of a comeback as it was no longer threatened by Franco Harris.

When a career in announcing and movies didn't pan out, he tried various other junctures such as in 1988 when he founded the Amer-I-Can Program. He currently works with juveniles caught up in the gang scene in Los Angeles and Cleveland through this Amer-I-Can program. It is a life-management skills organization that operates in inner cities and prisons. He is also a part-owner of the New York Lizards of Major League Lacrosse, joining a group of investors in the purchase of the team in 2012.

In 2008 while Brown was serving as an executive advisor to the Browns, he assisted to build relationships with the team's players and to further enhance the NFL's wide range of sponsored programs through the team's player programs department.

While all of this was splendid, the problem remains that no matter what good Brown did on and off the field, it was some of his antics and crimes that fans can never allow themselves to forget. His ex-wife Sunee Jones filed for divorce in 1968 and charged him with "gross neglect." Together they had three children, twins Kim and Kevin, and a son, James Jr.

Shortly before splitting with his wife, in 1965, Brown was arrested in his hotel room for assault and battery against an eighteen-year-old named Brenda Ayres. A year later, he fought paternity allegations that he fathered Brenda Ayres' child.

His issues with women didn't stop there, as in 1968, Brown was charged with assault with intent to commit murder after model Eva Bohn-Chin was found beneath the balcony of Brown's second-floor apartment. Yes, that's right—he dangled a woman from her feet from the second floor of the balcony. Brown was also ordered to pay a $300 fine for striking a deputy sheriff involved in the investigation during the incident. Later, Jim Brown would claim that it was all a big misunderstanding.

His issues with the law didn't stop at abusing women, however. In 1970, Brown was found not guilty of assault and battery, the charges stemming from a road-rage incident that had occurred in 1969. In 1975, Brown was convicted of misdemeanor battery for beating and choking his golfing partner, Frank Snow. He was sentenced to one day in jail, two years' probation, and a fine of $500.

In 1985, Brown was charged with raping a thirty-three-year-old woman. In 1986, Brown was arrested for assaulting his fiancée Debra Clark. In 1999, Brown was arrested and charged with making terroristic threats toward his wife. Later that year, he was found guilty of vandalism for smashing his wife's car with a shovel. He was sentenced to three years' probation, one year of domestic violence counseling, and 400 hours of community service or 40 hours on a work crew along with a $1,800 fine. Brown ignored the terms of his sentence and in 2000 was sentenced to six months in jail, which he began serving in 2002 after refusing the court-ordered counseling and community service.

He advised Ohio State standout tailback Maurice Clarett to leave Ohio State after just one year and try to turn pro, bucking the entire NCAA and NFL system. Clarett never recovered from the horrible guidance Jim Brown gave him, and ended up being a complete washout and spent time in prison as his own life spun out of control.

How fans who saw him play, teammates who played with him, and everyone who has studied the aura of Jim Brown choose to judge him is his or her own decision to make. No matter what he did off the field, no one can ever change what he did on it. It truly was the stuff of legend.

By the time he was done with the Browns, the list of accolades was a mile and half long.

Here are just a few of the stats and accomplishments that jumped off the page the most to me when I started breaking down his dynamic on field football career:

In just 9 seasons of professional football, Brown ran for 12,312 career yards, for an average of 1,368 yards a season when they were only playing 12 games per year.

He was drafted sixth overall in the 1957 NFL Draft out of Syracuse by the Cleveland Browns. He was easily the best running back in the NFL for his entire career before retiring prematurely to try his hand at Hollywood. He made the Pro Bowl all nine years he played in the NFL and was named to the NFL All-Pro team eight times as well. His single best game total of 237 rushing yards on November 19, 1961, ranks sixteenth all time for a single game total.

In 1963 he ran for 1,863 yards in a 14-game season. That averages out to 133 yards a game. If you multiply that output out over today's 17-game season, it equals 2,262. Basing that on today's current rushing record set by Eric Dickerson in 1984 with 2,105 yards, he would beat it.

In his entire career, he averaged 104.3 rushing yards per game, which ranks first all time. He is the only tailback in NFL history to average over 100 rushing yards a game for his entire career. That is unheard of by today's NFL standards and style of pass happy play.

Jim Brown currently sits eleventh all time in rushing yards with the 12,312 over 9 seasons in which most of the seasons were either 12 or 14 games each. Emmitt Smith played 15 years at an average of 1,223 yards a year for an NFL Career Record of 18,355.

If Brown would have played 15 years with his per season average of 1,368 per season times 15 seasons, his career would have finished at 20,520 yards for his career. We know Brown didn't, stopping after just nine seasons, but the amount of "what if" stats we can list off is mind boggling.

Jim Brown had 59 100-yard games during his career with Cleveland. The Browns went 50–7–2 in those games. It was the age-old adage that when your halfback goes for 100 yards, you win the game more times than not. Their winning percentage in those 59 games was 85 percent. It's also wild to think that Brown accumulated that many 100-yard games in only 9 years, that is an average of 6.5 100-yard games per season.

Jim Brown led the NFL in rushing in 8 of the 9 seasons in which he played. He had 126 total touchdowns in 118 career games which averages more than one touchdown per game, which is the highest ratio in the history of the NFL. His 5.2 yards per attempt for his career ranks first all time in the history of the NFL for RBs with a minimum of 900 attempts. He never missed a game, playing in every single one though his 9 seasons.

He is the first Cleveland Browns player to rush for 1,000 yards (1,527 in 1958).

He ranks 17th on NFL All-Time Rushing Attempts List (2,359).

He ranks 8th on NFL All-Time Rushing Yardage List (12,312).

He ranks 2nd on NFL All-Time Rushing Average List (5.219).

He ranks 4th on NFL All-Time Rushing Touchdowns List (106).

He was a 3-time NFL MVP in 1957 (his rookie year), 1958 and 1965.

NFL Rookie of the Year in 1957.

8x First team All-NFL 1957–1961 & 1963–1965.

8x NFL Rushing Leader 1957–1961 & 1963–1965.

5x NFL Leader in rushing touchdowns, 1957, 1958, 1959, 1963, 1965.

NFL Scoring Leader in 1958.

1960 NFL All Decade Team.

NFL 50th Anniversary All Time Team.

NFL 75th Anniversary All Time Team.

NFL 100th Anniversary All Time Team.

Bert Bell Award in 1963.

Number 44 now retired by Syracuse University.

Number 32 now retired by the Cleveland Browns.

*Final career rushing and receiving stats*

12,312 rushing yards

5.2 yards per carry

106 rushing touchdowns

262 receptions

2,499 receiving yards

20 receiving touchdowns.

Retired at 29 years old, right in his prime.

He has appeared in the following movies:

1964 *Rio Conchos*

1967 *Dirty Dozen*

1968 *Ice Station Zebra*

1968 *Dark of the Sun*

1968 *The Split*

1968 *Kenner*

1969 *100 Rifles*

1969 *Riot*

1970 *Tick, Tick, Tick*

1972 *Slaughter*

1972 *Black Gun*

1973 *The Slams*

1974 *Three the Hard Way*

1975 *Take a Hard Ride*

1977 *Vengeance*

1978 *Fingers*

1982 *One Down, Two to Go*

1987 *The Running Man*

1988 *I'm Gonna Git You Sucka*

1988 *Killing American Style*

1989 *Crack House*

1990 *Twisted Justice*

1996 *Mars Attacks*

1996 *Original Gangstas*

1988 *Small Soldiers*

1999 *Any Given Sunday*

2004 *She Hate Me*

2014 *Draft Day*

*All 59 Jim Brown's 100-yard games listed below:*

11/13/57 vs. Was 109 yards in a 21–17 win.

11/24/57 vs. LA for 237 yards in a 45–31 win.

9/28/58 vs. LA for 171 yards in a 30–27 win.

10/5/58 vs. Pittsburgh for 129 yards in a 45–12 win.

10/12/58 vs. Chicago Cardinals for 182 yards in a 35–28 win.

10/19/58 vs. Pittsburgh for 153 yards in a 27–10 win.

10/26/58 vs. Chicago Cardinals for 180 yards in a 38–24 win.

11/2/58 vs. New York Giants for 113 yards in a 21–17 loss.

11/16/58 vs. Washington for 152 yards in a 20–10 win.

12/7/58 vs. Philadelphia for 138 yards in a 21–14 win.

12/14/58 vs. New York Giants for 148 yards in a 13–10 loss.

10/4/59 vs. Chicago Cardinals for 147 yards in a 34–7 win.

10/18/59 vs. Chicago Cardinals for 123 yards in a 17–7 win.

10/25/59 vs. Washington for 122 yards in a 34–7 win.

11/1/59 vs. Baltimore for 178 yards in a 17–7 win.

11/8/59 vs. Philadelphia for 125 yards in a 28–7 win.

11/22/59 vs. Pittsburgh for 111 yards in a 21–20 loss.

11/29/59 vs. San Francisco for 114 yards in a 21–20 win.

12/13/59 vs. Philadelphia for 152 yards in a 28–21 win.

9/25/60 vs. Philadelphia for 153 yards in a 41–24 win.

10/23/60 vs. Philadelphia for 167 yards in a 31–29 loss.

11/13/60 vs. St. Louis for 173 yards in a 28–27 win.

11/27/60 vs. St. Louis for 132 yards in a 17–17 tie.

12/04/60 vs. Washington for 135 yards in a 26–16 win.

12/11/60 vs. Chicago for 100 yards in a 42–0 win.

12/18/60 vs. New York Giants for 110 yards in a 48–34 win.

10/22/61 vs. Pittsburgh for 114 yards in a 30–28 win.

10/29/61 vs. Saint Lous Cardinals for 109 yards in a 21–10 win.

11/5/61 vs. Pittsburgh for 110 yards in a 17–13 loss.

11/12/61 vs. Washington for 133 yards in a 17–6 win.

11/19/61 vs. Philadelphia for 237 yards in a 45–24 win.

12/17/61 vs. New York Giants for 102 yards in a 7–7 tie.

09/16/62 vs. New York Giants for 134 yards in 17–7 win.

11/25/62 vs. Pittsburgh for 110 yards in a 35–14 win.

12/15/62 vs. San Francisco for 135 yards in a 13–10 win.

09/15/63 vs. Washington for 162 yards in a 37–14 win.

09/29/63 vs. Detroit for 114 yards in a 35–10 win.

10/5/63 vs. Pittsburgh for 175 yards in a 35–23 win.

10/13/63 vs. New York Giants for 123 yards in a 35–24 win.

10/20/63 vs. Philadelphia for 144 yards in a 37–7 win.

11/03/63 vs. Philadelphia for 223 yards in a 23–17 win.

11/17/63 vs. Saint Louis for 154 yards in a 20–14 loss.

12/01/63 vs. Saint Louis for 179 yards in a 24–10 win.

12/15/63 vs. Washington for 125 yards in a 27–20 win.

09/27/64 vs. Philadelphia for 104 yards in a 28–20 win.

10/18/64 vs. Dallas for 188 yards in a 20–16 win.

11/01/64 vs. Pittsburgh for 149 yards in a 30–17 win.

11/08/64 vs. Washington for 121 yards in a 24–14 win.

11/15/64 vs. Detroit for 147 yards in a 37–21 win.

11/29/64 vs. Philadelphia for 133 yards in a 38–24 win.

12/27/64 vs. Baltimore for 114 yards in a 27–0 win.

09/26/65 vs. Saint Louis for 110 yards in a 49–13 loss.

10/03/65 vs. Philadelphia for 133 yards in a 35–17 win.

10/09/65 vs. Pittsburgh for 168 yards in a 24–19 win.

10/24/65 vs. New York Giants for 177 yards in a 38–14 win.

11/07/65 vs. Philadelphia for 131 yards in a 38–24 win.

11/14/65 vs. New York Giants for 156 yards in a 34–21 win.

11/28/65 vs. Pittsburgh for 146 yards in a 42–21 win.

12/5/65 vs. Washington for 141 yards in a 24–16 win.

# BIBLIOGRAPHY

NFL.com
Profootballreference.com
ClevelandBrowns.com
ESPN.com
KeeOnSports.com

# INDEX

# About the Author

VINCE MCKEE IS AN AUTHOR OF TWELVE PUBLISHED BOOKS AS WELL AS the CEO and founder of Kee On Sports Media Group, a company that is the leader in Ohio high school sports coverage and broadcasting.

McKee is a respected member of the high school football scene and has covered over twenty state championship games since entering the business in 2015.

Copies of his published work are sold all over the world. He has been featured on over twenty-five local radio programs as well as broadcast television, ESPN, Sports Time Ohio & Ballys Sports Ohio as well as several other news outlets for his previous work.

McKee travels the state giving motivational speeches about his start and experience in the business. When he is not calling or covering games, McKee is an avid pro wrestling fan. His favorite thing to do is spend time with his wife Emily and daughters Maggie and Madelyn.

If he is not watching sports, you will catch him watching documentaries about sports or the Food Network with his wife. As an avid Cleveland sports fan, he is living the dream as he has interviewed almost every single one of his sports heroes growing up from the 1980s and 1990s.

He can be reached via email at coachvin14@yahoo.com and twitter @SportsKee1.